FHM Presents...

THE BEST OF

BEACH
BAR
JOKES

This is a Carlton Book
Text copyright © 2006 Carlton Publishing Group and Emap Elan Network 2006

First published 2006 by Carlton Books
20 Mortimer Street
London W1T 3JW

ISBN 13: 978-1-84442-292-0
ISBN 10: 1-84442-292-5

Printed and bound in Great Britain

10 9 8 7 6 5 4 3 2 1

FHM Presents...

THE BEST OF

BEACH BAR JOKES

CARLTON
BOOKS

www.fhm.com/jokes

CONTENTS

INTRODUCTION

Jokes, jokes, jokes. That's what this book is full of. Long ones, short ones and everything in between. But this isn't just any old book of jokes. These gags have been specially selected for you when you're playing away from home. There are jokes specially for beach bars, jokes for when you're travelling, jokes for restaurants, nightclubs and hotels – there are even jokes just for you to use in even more exotic locations!

All of them were chosen to make you the life and soul of the party, so dig in, enjoy, and when you are taking credit and lapping up the laughs, remember to thank the world's greatest magazine – *FHM* – for everything!

CHAPTER ONE
Jokes about animals

Dicky bird

An American guy has been having a good time with the local girls in a poor country and he wakes up one morning with a growth on his penis. Alarmed, he goes to the doctor. The doctor (a family man with a lisp) knows about the wealthy American who's been bedding all the girls in town for money and decides to get rid of him. He has a look at the guy's genitals, hums and hahs and finally declares that he's suffering from chirpes.

"Chirpes? What the hell's that?" the guy exclaims, buttoning up his trousers.

"It's a bit like bird flu," the doctor explains. "It's a canarial disease and, I'm sorry to say, it's untweetable."

It makes sense

"Why is it always 'Women and children first'?" a female passenger asks at the captain's table. "As a feminist, I've always found this terribly patronising."

"Oh, it's got nothing to do with good manners," the Captain reassures her. "It's just that afterwards the sharks are full."

The cockatiel hour

In a zoo in Madagascar, an assistant zoologist has been working with the local population of parrots. She's leaving in the morning and the zookeeper warns the birds: "Tomorrow the assistant's leaving. I'll come round in the morning to help her pack and whatever you hear at the back, you keep to yourself. Do not – I repeat, do not – turn around and look at what we're doing there, otherwise I'll break your neck."

The birds can read between the lines and reluctantly agree; they've sussed out that the zookeeper has had designs on the assistant for a while and they can guess what's going to happen in the morning.

Unfortunately for the zookeeper, the assistant responds coldly to his romantic proposition and they end up simply packing at the back of the bird cage where she had her study.

They struggle with the equipment and, try as they might, they can't get the suitcase closed.

"OK, climb on top. It should work," the zookeeper tells the assistant. She climbs on top of the suitcase and, grunting and panting, she pushes as hard as she can, to no avail.

"Hold on," she says. "*You* go on top and give it a go." The zookeeper agrees and spends some time pushing and puffing and groaning – but the suitcase just won't close.

"Right," the zookeeper says. "Let's both go on top."

At this point one of the parrots turns around and says: "Neck or no neck, I've got to see this!"

Sex-starved

A guy is walking along in one of the dirt tracks they call streets in remote Africa. He's eating his sandwich when a chicken zooms past him, closely followed by a cockerel. The cockerel suddenly stops and starts pecking at the breadcrumbs which have fallen on the ground from the guy's sandwich.

"Man," the guy thinks. "I hope I never get *that* hungry."

No bull

A British tourist is visiting a ranch in Texas. He spends a week there, playing at being a cowboy, learning how to make a fool of himself with a lasso and all sorts of macho silliness. One day a new bull's being delivered to the farm and is moved to a pasture where ten or so cows are patiently waiting for him. All the cowboys are lined up along the fence to check out the bull, but are soon disappointed: the bull takes one quick look at the cows and deliberately turns away, gazing at the mountains.

"That won't do," one of the cowboys whispers to himself. "We'll have to get the vet."

The following day the vet comes round, checks out the bull and hands a jar of pills to the guy in charge. "Here you go. One of these morning and evening and everything will be fine." The cowboy thanks the vet and starts in with the medication.

The following day the British tourist is a bit late at the fence. When he finally arrives, he asks: "So how's the bull today?"

"He's doing great," the guy in charge says. "He's covered all the cows in this pasture already and he's working his way through the next lot. I guess these pills are effective."

"Yeah, I thought as much," the British guy says with a smile. "Still, I wish they had them in strawberry flavour."

File under 'Deceased'

A guy on holiday wants to buy a present for his girlfriend back home and decides on a canary. He goes to the local pet shop and asks for one.

"I'm sorry, sir; we've sold out," the proprietor apologises. "You see, the town's canary festival is coming up soon and I doubt there's a canary left to be bought. I do have a few parakeets, though."

"It's not the same as a canary," the guy grumbles.

"A parakeet can be made to sound exactly like a canary if you file its beak," the pet shop owner contradicts him. "All you have to do is to be careful not to file it too much, or it'll drown."

The customer is appalled at the idea, so he thanks the guy and gets out. He decides to try another shop. He gets exactly the same answer: there isn't a canary to be had in town because of the canary festival. "I do have a parakeet, though. If you file its beak, it'll sound exactly like a canary," the clerk at the second pet shop tells him with a patient smile. "Be careful not to file it too much, or it'll drown; that's the only thing to worry about."

This time, the customer takes the information a bit more seriously and considers buying a parakeet instead of a canary. Moreover, the parakeets are cheaper.

With his parakeet in a little cage, the guy heads for a hardware store to buy a file. There's quite a collection of files on display and the bloke doesn't really know which one to choose. An assistant walks up to him and asks if he can be of any help. Embarrassed, the guy shows him the parakeet and opens his mouth to explain what he needs, but the assistant cuts him off with an outstretched hand. "I have exactly what you need, sir," he says. He picks up a file from the shop and hands it to him, repeating once again that one has to be very careful with the filing, otherwise the parakeet might drown.

The following day the bloke is ready to head back home and

walks around the main street for the last time. The owner of the pet shop spots him and walks to him. "So, how's the parakeet? Have you filed its beak yet?"

"The parakeet's dead," the bloke answers.

"Filed it too much, did you?" the vendor asks knowingly, nodding.

"Oh, no," the bloke replies. "I didn't have time; it was dead when I got it out of the vice."

Shell hole

A tourist is on a discovery tour of Africa and has been led to a waterhole by a professional tracker. "Look," the tracker says in wonder. "All the animals come to drink here, their differences forgotten, united in the act of survival."

Just as he says these very grand words, an elephant spots a turtle drinking next to him. The tourist gazes in horror as the elephant jumps into the air and crash-lands on the turtle, reducing it to a gooey pulp.

"United, eh?" the tourist asks.

"Well, you see, I can explain," the tracker replies. "If I'm not mistaken, that turtle bit this particular elephant on the trunk some fifteen years ago. I remember it; I was there when it happened. And we all know what phenomenal memories elephants have."

"Fifteen years? Really?"

"Oh, yes," the tracker carries on. "We call it turtle recall."

Q. Why do seagulls live near the sea?
A. Because if they lived near the bay, they would be called bagels.

You don't have to be mad to work here...

A cow is sent to Great Britain and is finding the change a bit daunting. After a little while, though, she starts making friends with other cows.

"I'm quite worried about this mad cow disease," she confesses one day. "I mean, I heard a cow over at old McDonald's farm got it and she died horribly."

"Don't worry," another cow reassures her. "It doesn't affect us ducks."

Know the signs

While planning a visit abroad, you should always check what the Foreign Office has to say about the region you wish to visit. For instance, in the case of East Asia, the FO offers the following warning:

Bird flu is the major threat to which one can be exposed while visiting East Asia. If you suffer the following symptoms, you should see a doctor immediately, as it is a potentially fatal disease:

High fever
Nausea
Fatigue
Aching in the joints
An irresistible urge to shit on someone's windscreen.

Wet and wild

An elephant is strolling through the jungle when she gets a thorn in her foot. She's in absolute agony and she can't get to the thorn on her own; her trunk doesn't reach. By chance, she meets an ant strolling by and asks him for help. The ant says he will indeed help, on condition that the elephant lets him have sex with her.

"Anything! Anything!" replies the elephant.

The ant works for an hour, pulling the thorn out of the elephant's foot. As soon as the thorn is out, the ant is in, having his wicked way with the elephant.

Meanwhile, in a tree directly above them, a monkey has witnessed the whole episode and is in fits of laughter. He laughs so much, he falls out of the tree on top of the elephant.

"Ouch!" says the elephant.

"Yeah," grunts the ant, "take some more, bitch!"

Trunk and disorderly

What's six feet long and hangs from trees in Africa?
Elephant snot.

Simple when you know how

When on holiday in Africa, how do you make a dead elephant float?
Well, you take a dead elephant, one ton of chocolate ice-cream,
three tons of bananas...

Dust to dust

A bloke is on holiday in his rented cottage one lazy Sunday afternoon when he hears some crunching next door. Being nosy, he looks over the fence and sees his neighbour digging a hole in his garden. Naturally, he asks what the hole's for.

"My canary died and I'm burying it," says the neighbour.

"Oh, I'm sorry about that," says the bloke insincerely. He then has a closer look and adds: "That's a pretty big hole for a canary, though, isn't it?"

"Well, yes," replies the neighbour. "That's because it's inside your fucking cat!"

The long and the short of it

A family from New York buy a ranch out in the Wild West, where they intend to raise cattle. After a year or two, a friend finds the time to visit. He is greeted at the airport by his friend, who drives him all the way to the ranch. It's an impressive spread, with acre upon acre of land – all devoid of any animals. He decides not to comment on this, but instead asks about the family.

"Oh, everyone's fine," his friend reassures him.

"You're settled in here?"

"We're all perfectly happy," the rancher says with a smile.

"What did you call your place, then? I remember you had great plans when you left New York."

"Well, I wanted to call it 'Wild New York'," the head of the family laughs, "but the wife didn't really like it. She preferred 'Thousand Acres'. Sonny wanted to call it 'Ozzy Ranch' and little Danielle fancied 'Magical Ranch.'"

"So what did you call it then? Did you reach a compromise?"

"A compromise? With that lot? You must be joking... No, we ended up calling it the Wild Thousand Ozzy Magical Ranch."

"And... er... why don't you have any cattle? I remember you writing to say you'd bought some cows, or something."

"Yeah, well, they didn't survive the branding, actually," the ex-New Yorker says.

The beast in me

A family goes to visit Colchester Zoo for the day. They see the monkeys, the snakes, the antelopes, and after a while dad's had enough. He decides to retire to a nearby bench near the elephant enclosure.

"Mum, what's that?" little Johnny asks, pointing to the elephant.

"That's the elephant's trunk," she replies.

"No, not that; that!"

"That? That's the elephant's tail, dear."

"Not the tail: what's underneath the tail!" shouts little Johnny.

"Oh, that? Er... it's nothing," his mum replies, embarrassed.

Disappointed with his mum, little Johnny fetches his dad while mum sits down on the bench.

"Dad, what's that?" little Johnny asks, pointing to the elephant.

"That's the elephant's trunk," he replies.

"No, not that; that!"

"That? That's the elephant's tail Johnny."

"Not the tail: what's underneath the tail!" shouts little Johnny again.

"Oh; that's the elephant's penis. Didn't your mum tell you?"

"Nah," Johnny complains. "She said it was nothing."

"I'm really spoiling that woman," Dad says wryly under his breath.

19

Nature's way

A city bloke is visiting the countryside in search of potential clients. He parks on a side road to stretch his legs, gets out and leans against the fence. On the other side of the fence is an orchard, and there among the trees is a farmer with a couple of pigs. The man watches aghast as the farmer picks up a pig, lifts it up in the air and helps it eat the apples directly from the branches, moving it from one apple to the next. When the pig is done eating the apples on the left side, the farmer sets it back down on the grass and picks up the second pig, again carrying it at arm's length so that it can eat the apples.

When the little dance is over, the bloke walks over to the farmer and says: "I've never witnessed such a thing. That must be the most awkward way to feed apples to a pig. Don't you see you'd gain a fantastic amount of time just by shaking the tree to make the apples fall to the ground?"

The farmer looks him up and down and replies: "What's time to a pig?"

When push comes to shove

A family is on holiday in an activity camp when the little boy witnesses a dog shagging a bitch in the street. He turns to his dad and asks: "What's happening there, dad?"

The father is embarrassed and lamely explains that the bitch doesn't want to go back home and that the dog is pushing her.

"I see," says the little boy. "It's a bit like mum yesterday. It's a good thing she was holding on to the sink, otherwise the instructor would have forced her to go to the gym."

Cruel creation

An elephant meets a camel. He looks the weird animal up and down. then says: "Tell me; why is it you've got your tits on your back?"

The camel sniffs and replies: "That's a funny question coming from an animal who's wearing his todger on his face."

CHAPTER TWO
Jokes for Bars

Polly pulley

There's this bar on a beach which has a very nice bamboo décor, with palm trees behind the counter, reclining cane seats and a superb parrot on a perch.

This guy's been sitting at the counter for a while, sipping from a cocktail with a little umbrella in it. From time to time he glances at the parrot, only to be met with a baleful glare, as if the parrot were silently daring him to say something.

"Your parrot's the silent type, eh?" he remarks to the bartender after a while.

"That's because he only does requests. You see these two strings tied to his legs?"

"Yeah; I was wondering about them."

"Well, if you pull the left one, he'll sing a French romantic ballad."

"No way!"

"Give it a go; it's free," the bartender replies, waving to the parrot.

The guy turns around and rather gingerly stretches his hand towards the string, expecting the beast to bite his fingers off. Nothing happens, though, and, more confident, he grabs the left string and pulls. The parrot straightens up and delivers La Mer with a beautiful French accent.

"That's really good," the guy congratulates both parrot and bartender when the song's over. "And what does the right string do?"

"That's for Italian songs. We tend to attract quite a few foreigners in the evening," the bartender explains.

The guy nods, turns around and pulls the right string. The parrot sways on its perch with drama and starts O Sole Mio with gusto.

"This is truly amazing," the customer says with tears in his eyes when the songs ends. "And if you pull both strings at the same time, I suppose it'll sing Lili Marlene in German, right?"

The parrot replies, "If you pull both strings at the same time I fall off my perch, you stupid arsehole!"

The long view

A woman is served a cup of coffee on a hotel terrace. She takes one sip, makes a face and calls the waiter.

"This is probably the worst cup of coffee I've ever tasted," she complains.

"Be reasonable," the waiters says. "You may be old and weak yourself some day."

A taste of home

A man is waiting for his weekend date by the seaside, munching on a bun. It tastes really disgusting: so vile, in fact, that the guy decides to walk back to the bakery and complain.

"I'm sorry, but this bun is inedible. It tastes like a bar of soap," he complains.

"Er, yes," the girl behind the counter replies. "It's a Bath bun."

Doing his duty

Two middle-aged men are chatting at the bar. They're dressed as typical tourists – flowery shirts, absurdly out of fashion beach hats and clip-on sunglasses. They are talking shop.

"I only believe half of whatever people tell me," says the first man.

"Really? What do you do for a living?"

"I'm a psychoanalyst."

"Well, what a coincidence. As for me, I always believe twice as much as people tell me."

"Twice as much? What do you mean?"

"I'm a tax inspector."

Lessons for life

Sipping a nice cold beer while sitting in a deckchair on the white sands of Barbados must not prevent you from pondering the deep questions the human race faces. Sipping four or five beers might actually help you find some answers! So read the following statements and evaluate their philosophical value... before throwing this book in the bin and heading for the sea:

Familiarity breeds children.
I think... therefore I am confused.
Sometimes too much drink is not enough.
When all else fails, read the instructions.
If at first you do succeed, try to hide your astonishment.
Friends come and go, but enemies accumulate.
A penny saved is virtually worthless.
Don't lend people money; it gives them amnesia.
For every action, there is a corresponding over-reaction.

He who dies with the most toys is still dead.
Old age and treachery shall overcome youth and talent.
Anyone can admit they were wrong; the true test is admitting
it to someone else.
A short cut is the longest distance between two points.

It's all a blur

Two elderly tourists are sitting at a bar in Acapulco, watching the young Brazilian girls go by. One says to the other: "You know, I'm still sexually interested in women. In fact, I always get excited when I see the young girls walking by. The real problem is that at this age, I don't see so well any more."

Forbidden pleasures

A Catholic priest and an imam have been sent to a pan-religious meeting by their respective congregations. They meet at the bar of the hotel where the conference is taking place and have a drink.

"Come on; let's be honest," the priest says after a glass of wine. "Tell me frankly whether you've ever tasted a ham sandwich."

The imam contemplates his glass of orange juice and grins. "Yes, I have," he confesses. "I didn't really like it all that much and I felt sick. But what about you? You lot are supposed to be celibate; have you ever had sex with a woman?"

The priest looks around to make sure no one's listening and he, too, grins.

"Yes; once."

"Beats the hell out of a ham sandwich, doesn't it?" the imam replies.

A place in history

A youngster's visiting Wales on his motorbike. He's been driving for
an hour and decides to stop and have a spot of lunch in a pub. The
pub's quite crowded, so he has to share his table with an old codger
who looks at him with forlorn eyes.

"I remember when I first came to Wales," the old geezer says,
looking at the biker. "I was full of enthusiasm: full of ideas." He
points to a big hole in the side of a nearby hill. "See that? It was me
who started digging slate there. I was employing half the town, but
did they call me Harry the Digger? No: oh, no!".

The biker nods sympathetically, wondering where all this is
leading, and takes a sip of his beer.

"Then I used the money from the quarry to pay for the railway
tracks to be laid down so the town was connected to the rest of
the country. New horizons, access to art and new ideas and new
fashion. Our lads started going to university and making a name
for themselves in Birmingham and then London. Then we built the
concert hall and the theatre. Did they call me Harry the Builder? No,
they didn't, did they?"

The old man grumbles and shakes his head in resentment. "I fuck
one sheep ..."

Just plain vicious

A man is sitting at a table reading a newspaper over a cup of coffee
when a young woman sits at the table next to him. They nod
politely to one another, then nod again when the waiter shows up to
take her order and then again when he brings it. They smile at each
other and start a conversation. After a while, they're like old friends
and start being very open.

"I have to confess," the woman eventually admits, "I'm a bit of a
pervert."

The man's taken aback, but replies: "It's OK, I guess. I mean, none of us is really completely sane, you know. A little perversion is harmless."

"Oh, but if you knew!" the woman says with flaming cheeks.

"You can tell me," the guy reassures her. "I mean, we're two strangers. It's not as if I'm going to repeat what you say to people you know, is it? And anyway, I'm a pervert myself."

"You? I can't believe it."

"Oh, yes, indeed. Tell you what: you tell me what your perversion is and I'll tell you mine."

The woman thinks about it and agrees. "I like to be kissed on the bottom," she confesses.

"Is that all?" the man laughs. "That's nothing. Now, go to the men's bathroom and take all your clothes off. I'll show you my perversion."

The woman gasps and puts her hand to her mouth, but she agrees. She goes to the bathroom and takes her clothes off, hoping the guy's perversion has something to do with the kissing of bottoms. She waits fifteen minutes, half an hour and the guy doesn't show up. Incensed, she gets dressed again and returns to her seat.

"Where were you?" she hisses. "You said you were going to show me your perversion."

"Oh yes," the man replies contentedly. "I just crapped in your handbag."

Too much information

Two families are sitting down at the campsite bar, doing the crossword together. They're stuck on the clue, "Centre of female pleasure (8)."

"Clitoris," says one of the husbands, suddenly inspired.

"How do you spell that?" the other husband asks.

"Can't remember. You should have asked me last night; it was on the tip of my tongue," he replies, to his wife's total embarrassment.

War of words

Everyone's on holiday. The streets are empty, the offices deserted, and in the bar it's very quiet indeed. A guy walks in and sits down. He's the only customer.

"What can I get you?" the barman asks.

"Make it a large Scotch," the customer says.

The barman serves him a drink which the customer gulps down with obvious satisfaction. To the barman's surprise, he then gets up and starts to leave.

"Oi; that's £4.50," he says angrily.

"Actually, it isn't," the customer replies calmly. "You see, you asked me what I wanted to drink. It was an invitation, pure and simple, and at no time was there any hint that any kind of financial transaction was going to take place." The customer lights a small cigar and carries on: "You see, I'm a lawyer. I've made a study of such cases. I'm the only one who's not gone on holiday yet. If you pursue this laughable claim, I shall take you to court."

The barman is disgusted but he doesn't want any trouble, so he just tells the guy to sod off and never show his face in there again.

The following day, the same guy shows up.

"You've got some nerve, coming in here," the barman says menacingly.

"What do you mean?" the customer asks with a great show of surprise.

"What do you mean, 'What do you mean?' You're the guy who swindled a Scotch out of me yesterday."

"You must be mistaken; I've never set foot in here before," the guy says earnestly.

The barman looks deep into the customer's eyes and shrugs. "That's uncanny," he says. "You must have a double."

"Thank you very much. Make it a Scotch."

Taking a slash

A guy is visiting the gents'. He's going along his business when the man at the next urinal says: "I'm sorry, but I couldn't help noticing that you're circumcised."

"Er... yeah; I'm a Jew and I've been circumcised."

"And I'm pretty sure your rabbi was Rabbi Jacob, from Islington."

"You're right, actually. How do you know?" the guy asks, surprised.

"Rabbi Jacob never could cut straight; you're pissing on my shoes."

CHAPTER THREE
Exotic Jokes

Reaching the bottom

How do you know you've arrived in a Mexican barrio?
  You see toilet paper hanging on the clothes-lines.

The man in black

A missionary is sent to a remote village in Africa. He checks in with
his host, a vicar living in a mansion nearby. "Today is your first day
in your new parish," the vicar says. "I'll have my cleaning lady iron
your clothes, so you can look your best."

  Soon the priest is wearing a spotless black robe and an
immaculate white collar. Everybody in the village notices him, and
after a few minutes a man walks up to him.

  "Good morning, mister," he says: then, pointing at the white
collar, "Tell me, why do you wear your shirt backwards?"

  "That's because I'm a Father," the priest replies with an affable
smile.

  "Well, I'm a father too," the man reflects, "but I don't wear my
shirt backwards."

  "It's because I am a father of thousands," the priest explains
condescendingly.

The man looks at the priest in disgust and says: "Well, maybe it's your trousers you should wear backwards!"

Off the beaten track

Three men are touring South America as part of an adventure package holiday. One is American, one is French and the other one is English. On the fourth day of their visit, their minibus crashes and they find themselves in the jungle, disorientated, bruised and hungry. It doesn't take them long to get hopelessly lost and to trespass into the secret territory of the Amazon Indians.

They've been plodding along bickering for a couple of hours when they're suddenly seized by a small party of fierce-looking warriors, armed with spears and their faces marked with scary tattoos. They are marched to the centre of a small hidden village and are swiftly tried. The punishment for trespassing is usually death, but seeing they're foreigners and didn't do it on purpose, they get sentenced to thirty lashes instead.

"It is our law that you may have something on the skin of your back to help you numb the pain," one tribesman says in broken Portuguese.

The Englishman, who's going to go first, asks for oil. An Indian applies oil to his back and all through the flogging. Despite the oil, the Englishman ends up on his knees and has to be carried away. The America, going next, is rather pale, but he straightens up and declares that he won't take anything. If he was hoping to impress the Indians by his bravery, he fails miserably: they just shrug and lash away with as much gusto as they did with the Englishman.

While the American is dragged to the side, where he collapses next to the Englishman, the Frenchman had his shirt ripped off by a tribesman.

"Will you take something on your back?" one asks him.

"Yeah; I'll take the American."

No job too large

An American is visiting the red light district in Amsterdam and has just been given a fantastic blow-job, but is surprised to see the prostitute spit his gift into a jar kept under her bed.

"I thought you lot liked swallowing the stuff," he remarked.

"We do," the prostitute deadpanned. "It's just that it's the weekend soon and we've got a bet running. The one who's got the most gets to drink it all."

Waste not, want not

Two men and a woman find themselves shipwrecked on a desert island. They have no shelter, no food – nothing. The woman soon becomes so depressed that she climbs to the top of a cliff and hurls herself off into the surf. The men, not surprisingly, become depressed themselves and bury her in the sand. After a week, they're even more depressed, so they dig her up again.

The way to the top

The Prime Minister is on holiday in Italy, being entertained by his Italian counterpart in a palace full of venerable and expensive-looking paintings, golden chandeliers and heavy carpets – not something that would ever happen in real life, of course.

"How do you manage to afford such a place?" Blair asks Berlusconi.

"See that motorway over there?" Berlusconi asks, pointing out of the window.

"Yes; so what?"

"The motorway cost 20 million euros. I charged 22 million and pocketed the difference," Berlusconi replies smugly.

Blair nods approvingly and returns to Cherie and a lobster dinner.

A few years later, it is Berlusconi's turn to be invited to Great Britain on holiday. He's picked up from the airport by helicopter and whisked off to a castle set amid lush, rolling acres. The castle is full to the brim with works of art, old and new, there is marble and gold everywhere and his suite is imperial. At dinner-time, sitting around a table that could easily have easily accommodated King Arthur and his knights, their retinue and their horses, Berlusconi is served a sumptuous dinner.

"I see you've moved up in the world," he congratulates Blair. "I take it you've given some thought to what I told you the last time we met?"

Blair remains silent, but his face splits in a wide grin. He stands up, beckons Berlusconi to follow him to the window and whispers to the Italian PM: "You see that motorway over there?"

Berlusconi frowns and replies: "No."

Grand slam

It's the end of the holidays in a family resort. Two blokes have become close friends together and have spent their time womanising and sleeping around. On the last night, one says to the other: "You know, apart from my two sisters and my mother, I think I've screwed all the tarts available in here!"

"That's great," the other replies. "Between us, we got the lot!"

An awful warning

A guy is walking home after work one evening when he's stopped by a homeless bloke asking for money. The sky is blue, the air is nice and crisp and the guy feels charitable. He opens his wallet and takes out a fiver.

"You're not going to use this to buy some beer, are you?"

"Nah," replies the bum. "Drinking's what brought me to this state. I haven't had a drink for years."

"You're not going to go to see the girls, either?"

"No way! I won't risk any disease for a fiver, man."

"What about football? You're not going to spend it going to see a match, are you?"

"No, I don't follow the football any more. I just want to get some food, is all."

The bloke puts the fiver back in his wallet and his wallet back in his pocket.

"Tell you what; I'm going to take you home," he says to the stunned vagrant. He picks up his mobile phone. "I'm just warning my wife."

"You can't do that to her," the homeless guy says. "I'm all dirty and I don't smell too good."

"Don't worry; you'll be perfect," says the man. "I just want to show my wife what a man who's given up beer, sex and football looks like."

Mind over matter

A woman's on holiday with her husband and has been plagued by blinding headaches. It could be the Spanish heat, or maybe something she ate. In any case, she's got to do something about it or it'll ruin their holiday. The tablets ordered by the doctor don't seem to be very effective and she's a wreck at the restaurant, her face dropping into her plate. The waiter approaches and enquires: "The lady is not feeling well?"

"She's been suffering from a headache for three days," the husband explains.

The waiter nods in understanding. "It does happen. Tourists sometimes can't take the climate." He gives the husband a business card. "This is my cousin Paulo. He's a hypnotist. He's treated people with your wife's ailment many times before."

The husband thanks him and, the following day, takes his wife to the hypnotist. He doesn't really think it'll work, but he's willing to give it a go if it has the slightest chance of salvaging the rest of his holiday.

His wife goes in and he settles down for a long wait over an old magazine, but she's back out in minutes, looking like a different woman. "It worked!" she explains. "He placed me in front of a mirror and I had to repeat "I don't have a headache; I don't have a headache" until it went away."

The bloke thinks about it all the way back to the hotel where, confident that his wife once more feels receptive to his sexual advances, he picks her up and deposits her carefully on the bed. "Don't move," he whispers, and disappears into the bathroom. He comes out ten minutes later and makes passionate love to her. As they lie in each other's arms, he smiles and says: "Don't fall asleep; I'll be back in a minute." He vanishes into the bathroom once more and, when he comes back, he's full of stamina again and treats his wife to more great sex. After the third go the wife, very pleased but quite tired now, quietly follows him to the bathroom. Her husband is standing in front of the mirror, staring at himself and repeating: "That's not my wife; that's not my wife."

Be sure your sin will find you out

A religious woman is visiting Scotland. One day she rushes into a church in tears and dashes to the confessional.

"Oh, Father, the waiter at the bar in the village is a fucking bastard!"

The priest is taken aback. He knows she's on holiday in his parish and had thought she was a respectable woman.

"Come on; you can't just say that."

"Oh, yes, Father; he's a fucking bastard!"

"But why? What's he done to you?"

"He put his hand on my knee!"

The priest opens his door and comes to sit next to the woman.

"See? I also put my hand on your knee and I'm not a fucking bastard."

"Well, no: but he put his hand underneath my skirt."

"Well, so do I, but that doesn't mean I'm a fucking bastard."

"Then he slid his hand up my thigh."

"Like this? So what? That doesn't mean he's a fucking bastard."

"But then he put his hand in my knickers."

"I'm putting my hand in your knickers myself now, and I'm not a fucking bastard."

"Then he took out his big... his big... and put it inside me!"

"That doesn't make a man a fucking bastard," the priest says, beginning to hump the woman for all he's worth.

"Yes: but then he told me he had Aids!"

"Ahh, the fucking bastard!"

Mug's game

A blonde has decided to go on an educational holiday. She's booked herself on a tour of Russia to visit the mines, the cement factories, the Olympic gyms and the like. One day she finds herself on a trip to a psychiatric hospital, being given the grand tour by a friendly man in a white coat.

"Here is the final stage of our treatment," he says at the end, indicating a bath full of water. "When we think a patient is well enough to rejoin society, we bring him here and ask him to empty the bath." He points to a cabinet on the side, full of different-sized mugs. "Then we ask him to pick one of these mugs."

"I see," the blonde says. "If he's feeling well again, your patient takes the biggest mug, right?"

The doctor looks at her curiously. "No, young lady; if he's well enough, he pulls out the plug."

An alarming discovery

Two girlfriends have been staying late in a Paris bar without their hubbies. They've been drinking all night and now, on their way back to the hotel, they're dying for a wee. There's nowhere to go, though, except a cemetery. They glance at one another, giggle and decide to go on a tombstone. The first one, having nothing to wipe herself with, decides to use her knickers and to throw them away afterwards. The other retains hers, but wipes herself with a wreath she's found on the grave.

The following morning, their husbands meet over breakfast.

"I think we should keep an eye on our wives," says the first. "Last night mine came home without her knickers."

"You're telling me we should; mine had a card stuck up her crack reading, "We'll never forget you, with fondest regards from all the lads at the fire station."

Alphabet soup

An Englishwoman is shopping for a new bra in an Italian supermarket. She's completely confused by the way sizes are displayed in Europe. As far as she can see, the bra sizes range from A to F, but she's got no idea how they compare to those in Britain. She stops a passing sales assistant.

"Oh, the sizes are quite easy," the assistant replies in passable English. "A is for Adorable, B is for Big, C is for Crazy, D is for Devilish, E is for Enormous."

"What's F then?"

"F is for Fake, Signora," the girl answers.

A stroke of good fortune

Husband to wife: "Honey, I won the lottery! Grab your suitcase!"

"Which one, the summer one or the winter one?"

"Both, you're out of here!"

Bottling happiness

A couple are on holiday in Moscow. The husband has been sampling the local vodka all night in a clandestine bar somewhere and he's now completely plastered. He's swaying through the streets, occasionally kicking aside an empty bottle. As luck would have it, one of these bottles contains the inevitable genie.

"Thank you from releasing me from my prison," the genie says. "I will give you one wish."

The bloke stares at the genie and says; "I want to be able to get drunk any time, anywhere. Change my piss into vodka!"

The genie makes a face, but agrees.

The following day the bloke wakes up with a terrible headache. He goes to the loo and realises that his urine smells of vodka. Stunned, he realises what he'd thought was an alcohol-fuelled dream might actually have happened. He picks up the glass he uses to rinse his mouth and pees in it, just to be sure. He sniffs the liquid and, very slowly, has a sip. It's vodka: no doubt about it. Radiant with happiness, he goes back to his wife in bed and explains the whole thing. His wife's dubious at first but agrees to have a taste from the glass. To her enormous surprise, it is indeed vodka. The husband, his headache forgotten, drains the glass and serves himself another one, which he drains in one gulp again.

"Hey – you could at least offer me another glass," his wife says.

"No need," the husband replies, stretching out on the bed. "You'll be drinking from the bottle."

In the stars

There is a deep inner need, for some people, to have their fortune told while on holiday. This particular woman is no exception and she ends up, with a friend, seated at rickety table, candlewax dripping on her skirt, listening to the rambling of an old hag wearing a headscarf, loads of bangles and a shrewd expression.

"You will soon be contacted by the authorities," she says, "maybe someone from the tax office? Oh, yes; I see money involved in the cards; you will be asked to pay quite a lot soon."

"Oh no!" the woman exclaims "I completely forgot to fill in my tax return form before leaving!"

"Don't worry about it," the seer carries on. "You won't have to pay anything. I can see a fatal accident with a bus two days before you go home."

The white stuff

Over a drink in a hotel bar, a Frenchman, a Japanese and a Dutchman are talking about milk. As you do.

The Japanese man says he prefers soy milk, because it's healthy.

The Dutchman says he prefers untreated milk, straight from the cow's udders, because it has more taste that way.

The Frenchman says he prefers woman's milk.

"Woman's milk? Why? You're not a baby," asks the others.

"I just like the packaging."

Q. What's the difference between the tax office and a new secretary?
A. The tax office will suck you dry.

May and December

An old man is sitting on a bench in a park, sobbing to himself. A tourist passes by and, reluctant to have his wonderful holiday spoiled by a bad memory, he walks over and sits down next to him.

"What's the problem? Can I help?"

The old geezer lifts his red-rimmed eyes, pulls his handkerchief out of his pocket, blows his nose and replies: "Thank you, but I don't think you can. You see, I'm in love with a 20-year-old girl."

"Ah, well..." the tourist says, awkwardly.

"You don't understand. You see, in the morning, when we wake up, we make love. She then cooks breakfast and we eat it in bed. Once breakfast's over, we make love again. At lunchtime, if she's not too busy, she comes back home to give me a blow-job. Then we make love again when her shift's over. We have dinner, we watch a bit of football on TV and then we go to bed and make love all night."

The tourist's dumbstruck. "What's your problem then? You seem to be having a great life."

"I've forgotten where I live!" the old man howls.

We gotta get out of this place

Two colleagues are desperate for a holiday. Their jobs are boring, the sun is shining outside and the gleaming thighs of the young secretaries topping up their tans in the park at lunchtime are more than flesh and blood can stand.

"I've had enough," said the first guy. "I know it's not ethical and I don't like to skive off, but I really need a break."

"How are you going to do it? You know we've got a tight deadline for this damned project," says his friend.

His colleague says nothing. Instead he climbs on to his desk, removes a couple of ceiling tiles, climbs through the hole, lies on the false ceiling and lets his head flop down through the hole. The supervisor arrives shortly afterwards and stares at him. "What are you doing there?" he asks, flabbergasted.

"I'm a lamp," the guy replies in a morbid tone. The boss is taken aback, then says: "You've been working too hard. Go home and have a rest."

Hearing this, the second guy picks up his jacket and prepares to leave.

"Where are you going?" the boss demands.

"I'm sorry," he says, "but I can't work in the dark."

Two sides to the story

A husband has a few days off and he's got some time on his hands. He decides this is an ideal opportunity to have a good look at his life, and he writes a letter to his wife to unburden himself.

"Dear wife.

I have something to say to you. I'm not happy with the way things are going between us. I've tried to make love to you 365 times this year and been constantly rejected. The reasons you gave me were as follow:

> We're going to wake up the kids: 34 times
> It's too late: 15 times
> I'm too tired: Five times
> It's too early: 52 times
> You pretended to sleep: 49 times
> The neighbours will hear us: Nine times
> Backache: Twice
> Headache: 26 times
> Sunstroke: Ten times
> My mother will hear us: 36 times
> I'm watching TV: Seven times
> I don't feel well: Nine times
> I don't feel like it: 21 times
> I've been to the hairdresser: Six times
> I'm having my period: 14 times
> I need the toilet: 19 times

The 36 times we did manage to have sex together weren't really satisfactory because:

> Six times you laid down and didn't move a muscle
> Eight times you heard noises in the loft
> Four times you asked me to hurry up
> Seven times I had to wake you up to tell you I'd finished
> and at other times I was concerned I'd hurt you because I felt you move."

The wife receives the letter stoically and nothing is said about it until the husband receives a reply from her one morning:

"Dear husband,
I fear your memory might be failing you. I have another explanation as to why we didn't have as much sex as you wanted last year. These reasons are as follow:

You came in drunk and tried to fuck the dog: Seven times
You didn't come back home at all: 29 times
You didn't manage to ejaculate: 14 times
You ejaculated very (actually *too*) early: 26 times
You ejaculated before entering me: 18 times
You ejaculated in your pyjamas while reading a porn magazine: Eight times
You had cramp: Nine times
You were working too late: 52 times
You had a skin rash, probably caught from the toilet seat: 21 times
You got into a fight and got kicked in the balls: Four times
You caught your penis in your fly: Eight times
You had a cold: 14 times
You had a very badly placed spot: Four times
You got your legs caught in the bed sheets and got irritable: Eight times
You were so drunk you went into bed the wrong way around and got kicked in the face while trying to kiss my feet: Eight times
You forgot about it as soon as you came back home: 25 times.

When I lay on my side not moving, it was probably because I was changing the bed. I never said anything about the loft: I asked you whether you wanted me on the front or on the back. I did ask you to hurry up a few times, but you have to understand I don't really like being smothered with farts. It is true that I have been tired recently though. This is caused by the frequent visit of the Alcoholics Anonymous representative whom I asked for advice about your behaviour and who now comes and sees me regularly."

Just plain ridiculous

Three blokes are talking about how stupid people can be, particularly women.

The first man says: "My wife just went to this designer shop and got herself a £500 dress she can't even get into."

"That's nothing," shrugs the second guy. "My wife just bought a new Mercedes and she doesn't even have a driving licence."

"Well, I guess my wife must be the most stupid of them all," the third guy says. "She's just bought a packet of 100 condoms before going on holiday to Mexico for a week, and I'm not even going with her!"

Dirty old men

A tourist overhears three old men talking on a bench.

"When I fart, it doesn't smell," says the first old geezer.

The other two say nothing for a while and then the second oldie says: "When I fart, no one can hear it."

The other two old men nod and remain silent for a little while and then the last one says: "When I fart, you can't smell it and you can't hear it either." The others remain silent for a while and then one of them turns slowly to face his friend and asks: "Why do you fart, then?"

Talk's not cheap

A guy is having a Turkish bath when a mobile phone rings. One of the other clients picks it up.

Everyone in the room can hear a woman's voice on the line

shrieking: "Oh, honey, I love you! I love you so much! I just walked pass this shop – you know, the one that sells fur coats? Oh I love you so much, I know you won't say no! I saw such a beautiful coat..."

"How much is it?"

"It's on sale, sweetie: only £1,500 – a real bargain! I'm sure you'd love me wearing this coat!"

"OK, OK, I love you too; you can get your coat if it makes you happy."

"Oh, I *knew* you'd say yes," the voice gushes. "And you know what? They have sales at the Mercedes dealership too, my love. I know you've always wanted a Mercedes convertible, but you've never had time to buy one."

"But honey, we've got cars already; we don't really need another one."

"It's on *sale*! It's black and it's only £23,000, all options. It's absolutely lovely!"

The bloke laughs. "All right, then. Get it for me. We can afford it."

"Oh, and before I go, sweetheart, you remember you asked me to go to the estate agent? I went this morning and they have a fantastic place on their books: twelve bedrooms, three reception rooms, lots and lots of character, 20 acres of land. He showed me some pictures; it looks absolutely ravishing. I'm sure Mother'll like it too. I have to phone them up later today to say whether we're interested, my love."

"Well, we do need a new place, don't we?" the bloke replies. "How much is it?"

"Around £2 million: a real bargain, apparently. You know how expensive property's getting round here."

"Go for it, honey. It's an investment."

"Oh, I love you; I love you. I just *love* shopping with you. 'Bye!"

The bloke switches the phone off, looks round at the astonished faces of his fellow-bathers and says: "Whose phone is this?"

C'est la vie

Five French tourists are talking in a hotel bar about what it means to be French.

"French people, above all, are polite," one says. "If a Frenchman were to come home and find a man in his bedroom wardrobe, he'd simply close the door again."

"This is true," the next agrees. "Although I'd add that if a Frenchman did find a man in the wardrobe, he'd say 'Good evening', *then* close the door."

"Exactly," the third says. "To be perfectly polite, though, if a Frenchman were to find a man in the wardrobe, he'd say 'Good evening' and then close the door only after having offered the man a glass of wine."

"You're right there," the fourth tells his neighbour. "Though you might argue that strictly speaking, a Frenchman who found a man in the wardrobe ought to say 'Good evening' and close the door, having offered the man a glass of wine, but then simply ask the couple to carry on whatever they were doing before he interrupted them."

The last guy nods and says: "I agree: but it seems to me that the really French way of life is to do all that, but then to stay and watch them at it."

The unkindest cut of all

A wealthy tourist in Cambodia has been with all the prostitutes around and, despise having taken all possible precautions, he finds himself with a very green and unhealthy-looking penis. He goes to the local doctor, who says the ghastly thing will have to be amputated.

"No way!" the guy declares. He goes to see another doctor, then another. He even finds a Western doctor and they all say the same thing: the old chap will have to go. Dejected and drunk, he's slouched at the hotel bar, pouring out his tale to the barman, when an old Chinese guy comes over and pats him on the shoulder. "I know a doctor who can help," he says.

The tourist is a bit suspicious, but he's got nothing to lose, so he agrees to follow the old Chinese geezer. He takes him to a derelict house in the poorest part of town where he's presented to an even older-looking guy who asks him to drop his trousers. The old Chinese doctor has a good look. "Wang not have to go!" he says with a toothy smile.

"You're sure?" the tourist exclaims.

"Yes, yes; soon will come off on its own!"

Spit it out, man!

A bloke with a speech impediment is on holiday and has developed a massive crush on the girl behind the counter at the chippy. He's never talked to her; he's far too self-conscious. He simply sits on the esplanade wall and stares at her for hours.

He's nearing the end of his stay and feeling very low and useless. That night, standing in front of the full-length mirror in his bedroom, he frowns at himself and promises to go and talk to her tomorrow. He then spends the best part of the night practising asking for cod and chips without stuttering. It's a gruelling exercise but, fuelled by his infatuation and his determination not to make a fool of himself in front of her, he finally manages to say the words "One cod and chips, please" without stuttering.

The following day, his heart pounding, he approaches the waitress. He takes a deep breath and asks: "One cod and chips, please."

"Sure; open or wrapped?"

"Fu... fu...fucccking... b... b... bitch," he mutters and stalks out.

Hard act to follow

Mr and Mrs Smith have booked a week's holiday at a leisure park.
They do different things, the wife preferring to stay near the pool and
the husband looking for some exercise. One day the husband goes
for a game of tennis with Rico, the Italian instructor, and after the
game he goes for a shower. His opponent is soaping himself already
and the husband can't ignore the massive shlong he's sporting.
Seeing the admiration in the bloke's eye, Rico says: "Every night I
bang it three times on the bedside table. It makes it long and hard.
That's an old Italian secret."

The husband nods his thanks for the tip and goes back home.
When he comes back home, his wife's having a nap. He gets
naked and is about to get into bed when he remembers the
Italian's shlong-size-increasing secret. He approaches the bedside
table, hold his member in his hand and bangs it three times on
the table.

"Is that you, Rico?" his wife mumbles sleepily.

Watch your mouth

While on holiday, you will no doubt sit down and watch the local
honeys strutting by, and even attempt to talk to them. Be careful,
though, in this age when lawyers are a woman's best friend, and use
only politically correct language when addressing them.

A woman is not a 'screamer' or a 'moaner'. She is 'vocally
appreciative'.
She is not 'easy', either. She is 'horizontally accessible'.
She is not a 'dumb blonde'. She is 'a light-haired detour off the
information highway'.

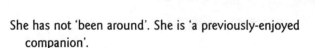

She has not 'been around'. She is 'a previously-enjoyed companion'.

She is not a 'airhead', she is 'reality-impaired'.

She doesn't 'get drunk' or even 'shit-faced'. She becomes 'chemically inconvenienced'.

She never 'nags'. She becomes 'verbally repetitive'.

She is not a 'tramp', but 'sexually extrovert'.

Equally, the same advice can be applied to ladies who fancy approaching the local blokes:

He does not have a 'beer belly'. He has developed 'a liquid grain storage facility'.

He doesn't 'get lost' all the time. He 'investigates alternative destinations'.

He is definitively not 'balding'. He has 'a follicular regression problem.'

He is not a 'cradle-snatcher'. He prefers 'generationally differential relationships'.

He doesn't 'fall over drunk'. He has 'an accidentally horizontal episode.'

He does not 'make a total ass of himself'. He develops a case of 'rectal-cranial inversion'.

He is not a 'male chauvinist pig'. He has 'swine empathy'.

He is not afraid of 'marriage'. He is 'commitment-challenged'.

He is not 'horny'. He is 'sexually focussed'.

He doesn't suffer from PMS, but from SRM: 'Semen retention migraine'.

And remember that what you'll be doing is not being 'unfaithful'. You'll just be involved in 'a concurrent, lateral, non-disclosed relationship'.

Heaven can wait

A man has died after a very dissolute life. He's been a drinker, a womaniser and an abuser of strange and illegal substances; in short, he's tried everything he's not supposed to do. On the other hand, he's left all his money to charity, so St Peter has a problem. Welcoming such a debauchee to heaven won't sit very well with some, but then again he's let in virtuous people who, while they didn't sin as much, ultimately didn't do as much good as this man either. He looks at the guy waiting at the Pearly Gates and finally gives him the key to Heaven, whispering: "I'll let you in, but I've got to warn you: you won't like it."

Nobody's perfect

Before having a lie-down for a couple of billion years, God created the Universe and saw that it was good.

He created Earth and saw that it was good.

He created Nature and saw that it was good.

He created the Animals and saw that it was good.

He created Man and saw that it was good.

He created Woman, and thought, "Well, she'll just have to use make-up."

Happy event

A couple of weeks after coming back from honeymoon, a woman goes to see her GP.

"Doctor, I think I'm pregnant."

"This is great news; congratulations. That fortnight in Goa wasn't wasted, then," he says with a confiding wink. The woman blushes and says: "It's marvellous; we're so thrilled. Since it's my first pregnancy, though, I was wondering..."

"Yes?"

"Is it really that painful?"

"Well, it depends on the woman, but as far as I know, yes, it is."

"How painful, doctor?"

The GP says: "Pick up your lower lip with thumb and index finger and pull."

"Like that?"

"Harder. Is it painful now?"

"A little," the woman says.

"Now pull your lip all the way around your head," the doctor concludes.

A brush with the Almighty

A priest needs his church painted. Because his congregation is poor, he looks around for the cheapest contractor. The one he chooses is an honest guy, more or less, but he needs to make a living and he decides that the only way he's going to make any money out of this job is to be economical on the materials. He mixes the paint with more turpentine than usual and applies only one coat. As is to be expected, the shoddy job doesn't last and a week later huge areas of the church are flaking. It looks absolutely ghastly. The priest is horrified and promptly sends a note to the contractor saying: "Repaint, repaint, and thin no more!"

Q. Why were most of Jesus' apostles fishermen and not cabinetmakers?

A. If they'd been cabinetmakers, Jesus would have had to say: "Drop your drawers and follow me."

You can suck my Dixie

It's Thanksgiving, and down in the Deep South old Mrs McDonald is feeling generous. Every year she cooks the best turkey she can get and asks over a couple of young recruits from the local garrison who are far from home to share it with her. As usual, this year she phones up the base.

"Fort Burnside; executive officer speaking."

"Good morning, Lieutenant. It's Mrs McDonald here. I'm having a little Thanksgiving party; I've roasted a turkey and I'd like to share it with two of your recruits who are far away from home, you know, to spread some happiness around in this festive period."

"Thank you for your invitation, ma'am," the lieutenant replies. "I'll find two recruits to keep you company tonight."

"Don't send any Jews, though," the old bigot orders. "I don't want any Jews in my house; is that understood?"

"Of course, ma'am. It shall be as you wish. I'm sure that I speak for the Army as a whole when I say we're proud to serve people with a good heart such as you."

The evening comes and the bell rings at the old McDonald place. At the door stand two black privates. One of them is holding a bunch of flowers for her. Old Mrs McDonald is understandably taken aback.

"Oh," says the old hag. "You're... you're... coloured people. I do declare there must have been a mistake."

"I don't think so, ma'am," replies one recruit. "Lieutenant Goldstein doesn't make mistakes."

Blood and fire

It's Christmas, and a Salvation Army brass band is playing in the village square. The song finishes and the conductor picks up a pot.

"Would you care to make a donation?" he asks an elderly lady.

The lady smiles and drops a fiver in the pot. The conductor nods in thanks and says: "Well, madam, for this money you can choose one of our hymns for yourself."

"Really?" she squeaks, delighted. "Give me... that one, the one playing the trombone."

A question of belief

A new priest is trying to do something to counter the evil tourism is causing to his flock. Now that public interest has been stirred up about little English villages and home-grown food, his congregation is either working hard to accommodate tourists or just lounging around in the square on Sunday mornings. As for the young people, they hardly get up at all on a Sunday after a busy night of fornication.

This particular Sunday is proving to be even more of a disaster than usual, as there is no one but a handful of drooling old fools listening to his sermon. After communion, the priest walks down to the town square and spots old Mrs O'Hara, sitting on a bench.

"What are you doing here, Maggie?" he asks, sitting down next to her.

"Well, I'm sorry, father, but the weather was so nice I thought I'd just enjoy a bit of sun instead of chilling my bones in that stuffy old church," she replies.

The priest is a bit taken aback, but he does see her point: the afternoon is very nice indeed; the air is warm and scented with the sweet fragrance of blossoming roses – altogether delightful.

"Don't you want to go to Heaven?" the priest asks her quietly.

"Oh no," she says, smiling.

The priest leaps to his feet and says: "Well, I'm ashamed of you!"

Now it is the old woman's turn to be surprised; then she says: "Oh, I thought you meant right now."

O little town of Bethlehem

A Jew, a Hindu and a born-again Christian have laboured long years to uncover the long-lost, heathenish secret of time travel. They all journey separately to a remote village in Italy, where some arcane signs guide them to a dank cellar, where the time machine has been hidden from the rest of the world for centuries. They all meet for the first time in this cellar and, as they're men of the cloth, they can't just murder the others and give all the glory of the discovery to their own faith. Instead they sit down around the machine, drink a drop of wine (apart from the Hindu) and decide to try it out, in case it's a fake. They agree to use the machine to go to Bethlehem and witness the birth of Christ.

They travel through time and space and, indeed, after a few stomach-churning moments find themselves in Bethlehem right before the birth of Jesus Christ. Unfortunately they're a little late and there's no space left at the inn apart from a small room, just enough for one guest: two if one of them doesn't mind sleeping on the floor.

"That's of no importance," the Hindu says. "I don't care for material goods. I'll spend the night in the stables."

A few minutes later the Hindu comes back. "I'm sorry," he says. "There's a cow in the stable. They're holy animals. I can't sleep next to a cow."

"No problem; I understand," says the Jew. "I'll go."

Ten minutes later the Jews is back. "I'm sorry," he says, shivering. "There's a pig in the stable and pigs are unclean to our faith. I can't sleep there."

"Fair enough," the born-again Christian says. "I'll go."

A few minutes later, a cow knocks on the door. "I'm sorry," she says, "but there's a born-again Christian in the stable..."

Keeping it dark

A woman has taken a couple of days off to have some quiet time with her lover while her husband is busy at work. Unfortunately, the husband comes back early from work one day and the woman has to hide her lover in the walk-in wardrobe. To his surprise and considerable irritation, the lover then discovers his mistress' teenage son has been hiding in there too, with a collection of men's magazines.

"Who the fuck are you?" the lover nearly shouts.

"Who the fuck are *you*?" the youngster replies.

"Never mind that; shut up."

The boy squints at the man but he can't make out his face.

"Dark in here, ain't it?" he says, without attempting to lower his voice.

"Shut up! And don't you switch your torch on, all right?"

"It's a nice torch, though," the boy says. "Wouldn't you like a torch like this?"

"I don't need a torch," the lover says.

"Oh, come on, I'm sure you do," the boy badgers, his voice subtly higher. Outside the walk-in wardrobe they can hear the husband's voice. The lover sighs. He's trapped; the boy's holding all the aces and all he can do is fork out and buy his silence. The lover pays up and leaves surreptitiously as soon as the coast is clear.

Later that week, the mother realises her son has been reading forbidden literature in the walk-in wardrobe. Although not really concerned about her own salvation, she insists her son goes to confession.

"Wow," the boy says, looking around the confessional. "It's dark in here. I wish I had a torch."

"Don't start that shit again," the priest says.

Dirty habits

Four young acolytes have spent a whole year in the convent under a vow of silence. Their lives have been strictly scrutinised and monitored, but now the Abbot thinks it's time for them to have a little bit of fun. He sees the four nuns in his office and tells them they're going to be allowed to let their hair down for one weekend only.

"Off you go, but remember to be back here in this office on Monday at 6am to tell me everything about your weekend."

Two days pass and the four nuns dutifully report to the Abbot's office bang on time. He instantly knows something's wrong. The four are shuffling their feet and avoiding his gaze. He groans inwardly to imagine what mischief they've been up to and asks the first nun what she's been doing during the weekend.

"Forgive me Father Abbot, for I have sinned," she blurts out.

"What is it?"

"I watched a X-rated movie with my brother. I think he was trying to be funny."

"I see. Well, these things happen. Just drink some holy water and return to your cell. We'll have a longer talk later." The Abbot turns his attention to the next nun.

"What did you do this weekend?"

"Forgive me, Father Abbot, for I have sinned."

"Yes?"

"I was driving my dad's new car and I accidentally ran over the neighbour's dog. I was so afraid of being found out that I pretended I didn't see anything and didn't confess later on that it was me who did it."

"That's not very nice, but it's not really a deadly sin. Drink some holy water and wait for me in your cell today." He faces the next nun.

"What about you? What have you been up to this weekend?"

"Forgive me, Father Abbot, for I have sinned."

"Yeah, yeah, yeah: out with it!" Out of the corner of his eye, he sees the last nun trying very hard not to laugh.

"Father, I ran naked down the High Street last night after my sister gave me a few glasses of vodka."

"Well, it seems you were all too weak to say no to temptation. It was to be expected; indeed, I expected worse than that. Go and drink some holy water and I'll have a chat with you later on."

The last nun is now howling with laughter and tears are pouring down her face. She has fallen on the stone floor and can't speak. The Abbot casts her a baleful look and, using his most stern voice, asks what she's done that's so funny.

"I pissed in the holy water!"

Eloquent silence

On holiday in Devon, a lad has met a girl he likes a lot. They exchange addresses when he leaves and both promise to write. Little by little, what could have been only a holiday fling grows into a fully-fledged love story and the girl finally asks the lad to come over and meet her parents.

"I've got to tell you, though, they're quite unusual," she warns him. "They're both deaf and mute, so they've devised their own way to communicate over the years."

The girlfriend takes his hand and leads him into the living room, where an effusive – if silent – welcome is waiting for him. The mum has prepared a delicious roast and they all tuck in.

All of a sudden the mother lifts up her skirt and shoves a bottle into her fanny. The dad shrugs and drops his trousers, puts his balls on the table-top and pushes his eyelids up with matchsticks.

"Mmmm, maybe I should translate there," the girl muses, seeing her boyfriend staring in disbelief at her folks.

"Mum just said: 'Get the beers in, you c**t', to which my dad answered: 'Bollocks, I'm watching the match.'"

Democracy in action

The town of Morons, in Nevada, is famous in America for its unusual voting methods. Instead of spending an enormous amount of money and lying to his constituents like all politicians do in the rest of the country, the post of Mayor of Morons will go to the candidate who can successfully perform four tasks: drink ten pints of beer, find a bear in a cave, shoot him down with a bullet between the eyes and have sex with an old, toothless Indian woman. Nobody would willingly go through such an ordeal, even a hardened politician, except that being the Mayor of Morons brings with it serious financial advantages.

The old Mayor has finally died and it's time for a new Mayor to be elected. All the contestants have been through the beer-drinking quite successfully, but none has survived the second task of finding a bear and shooting it down. The population is starting to despair when the village drunkard, after his fifteenth pint, decides to have a go at it. He lurches towards the mountains and disappears into the trees. After three days, he's back, his clothes in tatters, dehydrated, bloody and scarred. He crossed the main street before the awe-struck population, reels into the bar and says: "Somebody give me a beer – and show me this Indian woman I've got to shoot between the eyes."

Hairy moment

A young boy is visiting Amsterdam with his parents. Of course, there's no way they can avoid the red light district and the boy quickly gets some valuable insights into human anatomy.

Back home, his teacher asks the class to write a short paper on what they'd like to do when they grow up. He reads the boy's paper with concern.

"You want to be covered with hair when you grow up?" he reads in a disbelieving tone. "What on earth for?"

"Well, you see," the boy answers earnestly, "the women in Amsterdam only have a little bit of hair, but they make an awful lot of money with it!"

Q. What is the definition of something suspicious?
A. A nun doing press-ups in a cucumber patch.

Animal attraction

A couple are strolling down a quiet country lane, lost in one another's eyes, when they come across a bull mounting a cow in a field.

"What's the bull doing, honey?" the girl asks.

At a loss as to what to answer, the guy says: "Er... they're making pies, my love." The girl is satisfied with the answer and they carry on walking, until they come across a ram doing the business to a sheep.

"What about them? What are they doing?"

"Pies, Honey. They're making pies too," the bloke answers.

For the duration of their walk they stumble across all sorts of animals making pies: rabbits, horses, dragonflies... the bloke is getting hysterical and all this talk of pie-making has got him exceedingly horny. He turns to his girlfriend and asks: "Fancy making some pies too, darling?"

The girl acquiesces and soon he's shagging the living daylights out of her. When they're done, they resume their walk back towards the village. After a while, the girlfriend slows down and turns to face the bloke.

"I think the pie's ready now, sweetheart," she says.

"Oh yes? What makes you say that?" the bloke asks, puzzled.

"The gravy just ran down my leg."

Basildon blonde

Four Essex girls with behavioural problems have been on holiday in the north of Spain for a week with their learning assistant and now they're on the way back home. Unfortunately, their bus crashes and they're all killed. Because they're under-age, they go straight to see St Peter without having to hang around in Purgatory.

"Ah: a school group. Tragic, tragic," St Peter mumbles. "Now, all you need to do is to answer a couple of questions and you'll be on your way through to Paradise. First of all I'll need you name and age," he says to the first girl. She tells him her name. "Have you ever laid your hands on a man's thing?"

The girl giggles and replies: "Well, once I touched the head of one with the tip of my finger."

"No biggie," St Peter says. "Go and dip your finger in the holy water and go through." She looks at his paperwork and asks the same questions to the second girl: "Have you ever laid your hands on a male's thing?"

"Well, I once held one in my hands and stroked it," the second girl says.

"That's still acceptable," St Peter says. "Go and wash your hands in holy water and I'll let you through." The girl nods and saunters away.

Then St Peter sees the two remaining girls are having an argument.

"What seems to be the problem?" he says to the two girls.

"It's Tracy, Sir. She wants to push in first."

"Now, then, Tracy, there's no need to jump the queue," St Peter admonishes her. "We have all eternity here."

"It's not that," Tracy explains, frowning at the other girl. "It's just that if I have to gargle with holy water, I'd like to do it before Kelly-Jo dips her arse in it."

An eye for the birds

A guy is ambling along in Bangkok, eyeing the prostitutes in the windows. He's not usually interested in this sort of low-life, but the sheer quantity of sex on offer gets to him and he's getting the hard-on of his life. He spots a brothel with signs in English and goes in.

Instantly the madam is upon him and after his money. He tries to explain that all he's got is a fiver, as he hadn't thought he'd end up in such a place. With a shrug, the madam grabs his fiver, takes him to the back of the building and pushes him into a room. The place is bare. There's no furniture; no one's waiting for him. The only occupant is a chicken.

Pretty pissed off at having been swindled, the bloke considers murdering the chicken: but, as soon as his hands touch the lush feathers, an indescribable urge seizes him and he starts fucking the chicken. It's as if a door, closed for years, had suddenly opened in his life and the sex is absolutely fantastic.

He leaves the brothel exhausted, content and feeling vaguely guilty. Nonetheless, he's back the following day for some more clucking and pecking love, this time with a tenner in his pocket. The madam grabs his cash and leads him to a room. This time there are three other men in there, watching a couple having rampant sex through what appears to be a set of see-through mirrors. Forgetting his chicken, the man is instantly aroused by the show and blurts: "Wow; that's the best show I've ever seen."

"You should have been here yesterday," another bloke says, his eyes riveted to the spectacle. "They had a complete whacko in there screwing a chicken."

Q. Why are women such poor skiers?
A. There's not much snow between the bedroom and the kitchen.

I swear it's not rude

A gamekeeper strides out of his cottage and squints up at the sky. Today is going to be a fantastic day. Today is actually going to be a fishing day, he decides. He goes into his shed to pick up his gear and is on his way out when he meets the vicar.

"Come fishing with me, vicar," he says.

"I can't, my son," the vicar replies. "The Bishop's coming for dinner and I need to get ready."

"But it's only 11 in the morning!" the gamekeeper objects. "You've plenty of time. Come on; you seem tense. An hour of fishing will help you unwind." And he gives the vicar a friendly slap on the back to drive home his point.

The day's so nice that the vicar relents, accepts the offer and grabs a spare rod. Sitting in a folding chair, eyeing a float at the end of his line, he reflects that he has indeed been feeling rather tense and preoccupied recently, and that fishing is very relaxing. Suddenly, the gamekeeper shouts in surprise and leaps to his feet, wrestling with his rod. After battling for two minutes, he pulls a beautiful fish out of the water.

"Look at the size of that fucker!" he says to the vicar.

"Tom, it is indeed a very nice fish, but please mind your language."

"I'm sorry vicar, but this type of fish is actually called a fucker. I wasn't being funny or anything."

The vicar accepts the explanation and admires the fucker. An hour has gone by, though, and it's time for him to leave.

"Thank you, Tom. I had a great time. You were right; fishing is a very relaxing activity."

"Have the fucker, vicar," the game keeper says. "Cook it for your dinner and tell the Bishop it comes from your own waters."

The vicar thanks Tom and brings the fish to his cook.

"Here's a fucker Tom caught today. Could you dress it and cook it for the Bishop tonight?"

Hearing such profanity on the vicar's lips, the cook lets out a strangled cry and puts her hands in front of her mouth.

"I'm sorry," the vicar chuckles and then explains that the fish is actually called a fucker.

The Bishop arrives. He steps out of his limo and has a bored look around. The vicar takes him on a tour of the domain, to the pond and through the garden and they finally sit down for dinner.

"Tom, our gamekeeper, caught this fucker this morning," the vicar explains, "and I had it cooked for you tonight. Look at the size of this fucker!"

The Bishop stares at the vicar, his eyes wide and then a slow grin spreads on his face. He kicks his shoes off, put his feet on the table and start lighting a cigar. "You know, you bastards are alright," he says.

Blood on the carpet

Armed officers were called to a local housing estate last night after a man was shot in a row over a carpet. Police think it was rug-related.

She's got the hots for him

A sex-starved wife decides she's had enough, so she strips naked and waits upstairs for her husband to return from work. As soon as he shuts the door behind him, she rushes out of the bedroom and slides down the banister.

"What are you doing?" the husband asks, shocked.

"Warming up your dinner," the wife replies.

Read the small print

A bloke doesn't know what to buy his wife for her birthday.

"She's got everything she needs and anyway, when she does need something she just buys it herself," he moans to his friends at the bar.

"Why don't you give her something completely unusual?" one of them suggests.

"Such as what?"

"Well, I dunno... Wait, I read this article in a magazine; why not give her a voucher for 60 minutes of incredible sex, any way she wants? That's both a joke present and something quite cute, don't you think?"

The bloke thinks about it and finally nods. It would indeed make a great present and – who knows? – might lead to some nookie.

The following day the same bloke's back at the bar, looking glum.

"What's the matter? Did you offer her the present I suggested?"

"Yeah," the guy replies, throwing his friend a dark look.

"She didn't like it?"

"Oh no, she loved it! She read the voucher, kissed me on the forehead and dashed out of the house."

Q. Do you know why pubic hair's curly?
A. If it was straight, it'd poke your eyes out.

Have this one on me

A bloke goes to a brothel. He selects a beautiful girl and follows her into her room. £200 change hands and she starts undressing. Just as she's about to take off her bra and panties, the fire alarm goes off. The girl dashes out, still clutching the £200. The bloke swears, fumbles about with his clothes and runs after her.

The smoke's getting pretty thick and the heat's rising, so the man has to give up his search and instead approaches a fireman.

"Have you seen a girl in a red bra and panties coming out?" he asks him.

"Nope," the fireman replies.

"Well, if you see her, fuck her; it's paid for," the guy says, heading back to his hotel.

Her need was greater

A housewife has been for a walk in the market in Marrakech. When she comes back to her hotel room, she has the dubious honour of witnessing her husband enthusiastically shagging a young woman. To make matters worse, the girl's scrawny and doesn't seem too intelligent, either.

"Wait! Wait!" the husband shouts as she's ready to storm out. "I can explain. You see, there was this girl begging in the street. She looked so frail and tired... I took her to the hotel and fed her. You should have seen how much she ate! It was unbelievable. Then I noticed how dirty she was and I thought she could do with a shower or a bath, so I took her to the bathroom and ran some hot water for her. While she was in the bath playing with the bubbles, I had a look at the clothes she was wearing. They were hardly more than rags! So I rummaged through all the stuff you brought with us that you've never worn and gave her whatever you didn't use."

The man looks at the girl getting dressed in his wife's clothes. "She was about to leave, and then she asked: "Is there anything your wife doesn't use any more?", and so here we are..."

Age shall not wither him

An old man is a bit vain, because he's 70, but doesn't look it. He walks into a pub, orders a pint and asks the barman: "Guess how old I am!"

The barman thinks about it for a while and says, "50? 52?"

"I'm 70," says the old man proudly.

"Wow," says the barman, "I swear you don't look a day over 50."

Feeling extremely pleased with himself, the old man drinks his pint and leaves for the supermarket. He puts some groceries in a basket and heads for the checkout.

"Tell me," he says to the woman at the till, "how old do you think I am?"

The woman thinks about it and says: "50?"

"No!" laughs the man. "I'm 70!"

"Wow!" exclaims the woman. "You look great for someone your age. I hope I look as good as you when I'm 70."

The man pays and leaves. A short while later, at the bus stop, he goes for it once more.

"Tell me," he says to a woman who's arrived to wait for the bus too, "how old do you think I am?"

"Oh, I'm good at these games," says the woman. "I have a sure way to tell people's ages, but they have to show me their cock."

Things aren't going exactly as planned; the old man is a tad pissed off, but intrigued. He shrugs and drops his trousers. The woman cradles his old chap in her hand, pulls it, rubs it a bit while making thoughtful noises and finally says: "I'd say you're 70."

"How on earth did you know that?" the man says, crestfallen.

"I was behind you in the queue at the supermarket," she replies.

The Devil's work

An engineer dies and ends up at the Pearly Gates. Saint Peter checks his dossier and says: "There seems to be a mistake," so the engineer is sent to Hell.

Pretty soon, however, the engineer starts designing some improvements and upgrades to his living conditions. Soon Hell's got air-conditioning, flush toilets, escalators and mobile phones.

One day, God calls Satan up on the telephone for a chat. "So how's it going down there in Hell?"

"Things are great, actually," says the Devil. "We've got air-conditioning and flush toilets and escalators and stuff now. There's no telling what this engineer's going to come up with next."

"What? You've got an engineer? That's a mistake, I'm sure. He should never have got down there. Send him back up."

"No way," says Satan. "I like having an engineer on the staff; he's doing a great job here and I'm keeping him."

"Send him back up here or I'll sue!" says God.

Satan laughs uproariously and sneers: "Yeah – right! And where exactly are you going to get a lawyer from?"

Dream on, dear

In Rome, Stacy is staring admiringly at a Lamborghini. It's parked by an expensive-looking jewellery shop. Stacy breathes deeply and says to her friend Rose: "Wow; look at this car! That's exactly my type of man!"

Q. What's the definition of 'indecent'?
A. When it's in long, in hard and in deep, it's in decent.

European union

In an empty train carriage, a man is getting bored and lonely. Thankfully a young and smartly-dressed woman gets on and sits down opposite him. She smiles at him and picks up a thick report from her briefcase. The man's impressed by her very business-like demeanour and the way she purses her lips while reading what seems to be a very deep and difficult report. Out of sheer boredom, the guy glances at the title on the first page and is astonished to read the word 'penis'. The rest of the title is completely incomprehensible to him, apart from the word 'penis' typed in bold smack in the centre of the title.

He manages to remain silent for a full minute but finally blurts out: "I'm sorry to bother you, but do you mind me asking what that report's about?"

The woman smiles and says: "It's a pretty dry and boring report on the connection between human penis size and nationality."

"You mean there is one?" the man asks, astonished.

"According to this report, there is, yes," she replies. "As far as I can make out, the French penis seems to be the best. It has the widest circumference, which is the true factor as far as female pleasure is concerned. The German penis seems to be marginally longer. The British penis, on the other hand, doesn't really fare very well, I'm afraid."

"This is fascinating," the man says, extending his hand. "Let me introduce myself. My name's Pierre and I live in Berlin."

Drugstore cowboy

A stunning stud enters a pharmacy in London. He has powerful shoulders, long and sensual eyelashes, muscular legs: in short he's the kind of guy the sales assistant wouldn't mind a bit of a smooch with. She approaches him, looks him up and down and says: "May I help you?"

"I'd like some condoms," he says.

"Sure," the assistant replies, her voice faltering with desire. "What size?"

"Extra-large, please," the guy replies.

"Today's your lucky day!" the young woman says, breathlessly. "Today we're giving away free mobile phones with every purchase of extra-large condoms."

You'd better sit down

A young woman has just spent a week in Spain. Paella, sangria and local *cojones* have all put a strain on her system: she's actually more tired now than when she went, although much more relaxed. She goes to her GP for a check-up. The doctor runs a few tests and asks her to come back in a week.

A week later, he receives her in his office with a wide smile on his face:

"Well, Mrs Brown, I have great news for you..."

"It's not Mrs; it's Miss," the young woman says.

"Oh, sorry," the doctor says. "As I was saying, I have bad news..."

Natural justice

Two friends are busy getting drunk in a bar in Frankfurt.

"Tell me, if I sleep with your wife, are we friends?" says the first.

"No," the other replies.

"We're enemies, then?"

"No."

"What are we, then?"

"We're even."

Assault and battery

A little old lady slowly enters a sex shop, taking each step with painstaking care. Her movements are jerky and she looks as if she might fall to pieces at any moment. She hobbles the few feet across the store to the counter, grabs the top of the counter for support and asks the sales assistant: "Dddddooo yoouuu ssseeeellllll dddddiillllldddoosssssss?"

The girl behind the counter, trying her best not to burst out laughing, replies: "Yes, we do sell dildos. We carry all sorts of models and sizes."

The old woman then asks: "Dddddooo yyyouuu hhhave aaa ppinnkk onnne, tttteennn iiinchesssss lllllong aaaandddd tttwooo iinchesssss tttthicckkk?"

The clerk thinks about it, trying to remember all the models available and answers: "Yes, I believe we do."

"Cccccann yyyouuu ttttelll mmmeee hhhowww tttoo ttturnnn ttthe blooooodyyyyy ttthinggg offffffffffff?!"

Cutting to the chase

What a woman says: "Man, look at this place! C'mon, you and I need to clean up before my mum shows up. Look, your stuff is lying on the floor and you'll have no clothes to wear if we don't do the washing right now!"

What a man hears:

blah, blah, blah, blah, C'MON
blah, blah, blah, blah, YOU AND I
blah, blah, blah, blah, ON THE FLOOR
blah, blah, blah, blah, NO CLOTHES
blah, blah, blah, blah, RIGHT NOW

Clash of cultures

A Frenchman has been playing around with a stunning young woman during a business trip to Greece. After he gets home, he receives a letter from her telling him she's now pregnant and that her dad and her brothers are threatening to shoot her for bringing dishonour on her family.

The guy's a family man, but he feels the right thing to do is to confront the situation and to acknowledge his responsibility, so he flies out to Greece again. Now he is sitting in her family home, the target of staring and stony looks.

"Listen, I can't marry her, because I already have a family, but I don't want to let her down either," he starts. "We've both been careless and it wouldn't be fair if she was the only one to pay for our mistake. I'll tell you what I can do. I've done relatively well for myself. If she gives birth to a girl, I'll provide her with a house, a factory and £20,000 a year. If it's a boy, I'll double the annual income. If she gives birth to twins, I'll give them a house each. If she loses the baby… "

At this point the father, who has remained silent and stern-looking throughout the meeting, puts his hand on the businessman's shoulder and says: "If she loses the baby, you make love to her again."

Sixth sense

Two women friends are on the underground in Tokyo. The passengers are packed together like sardines. One of the women turns around to her friend and asks her: "Tell me; can you see the bloke behind me?"

"Sure."

"He's good-looking?"

"He's young," her friend replies.

"I can feel he's young," the other woman says. "I'm just asking if he's good-looking."

Every man's nightmare

A bloke collides with another bloke in an outdoor market in Tangiers.

"I'm sorry, mate," he apologises. "I've lost my wife in here; I'm looking for her and I guess I wasn't paying attention to where I was going."

"I've lost my wife, too," the other bloke says. "Maybe we could help one another."

"Sure. What does your wife look like?"

"She's tall, red-haired, green eyes, 25, quite busty and she's wearing one of those sexy tops that let the midriff show. What about yours?"

"Eh? Oh, never mind. Let's go and find yours."

The unwritten rule

A man, on the wrong side of 60 but still looking good, decides to forego his usual holiday in a rented cottage in Wales and instead opts for a beach hut in a nudist colony. He drives all the way to southern France, finds the holiday camp and pays his fee. He checks into his little hut, has a shower, starts to get changed but then remembers that he doesn't need to, and leaves the hut stark naked.

It's his first foray into nudism and he's got problem getting his erections under control. When a blonde bombshell walks directly towards him, he can't control it any more and just stands there, covered in shame.

"Did you call me?" the woman says.

"Er... no," the man replies, wishing he was wearing three layers of clothing and a waterproof coat in Wales.

"I think you did," she says, pointing at his erection. "This is the rule of the camp; if a man wants a woman, she's not supposed to say no. So: your hut or mine?"

The guy can't believe it. Tentatively, he nods towards his hut.

The woman, sensing his shyness, laughs gently, takes his hand and guides him to her own hut, where they spend the rest of the day shagging like rabbits.

The guy is now exhausted and he's lying in bed on his own, the gorgeous woman having gone for dinner. Thinking of dinner triggers the release of a string of farts.

"Did you call me?" a man's voice says just outside the window. The man stands up as a huge guy enters the room.

"Er, no," the man says, feeling cold sweat running down his spine.

"I think you did," the intruder says. "It's the rule of the camp that when a man wants to be taken, all he has to do is fart."

"Is that so?" the man asks feebly, ready to bolt.

However, he's no match for the muscular bloke and the rest of the night is spent in getting thoroughly sodomised.

The following day sees the tourist at the gate.

"Don't you like the camp, sir?"

"Oh, it's a cracking camp all right," he answers bitterly, "but you see, at 64 I get an erection every six months, but I've been farting in bed ever since I was twelve."

One of those nights

John's been to the pub and he's now back home, swaying on his feet, trying to find his way to the bedroom. Frightened that his wife might be very angry indeed at seeing him in this state, he decides to gargle some lemon juice, to make the stench of beer go away. He picks up a lemon, squeezes it and, although his eyes water, he drinks the whole lot before going to bed.

The following day he's rudely awakened by his wife.

"You've come back shit-faced again!" she accuses him.

"No, honey. Smell my breath; it doesn't smell of beer, does it?"

"And the squashed canary? It committed suicide, did it?"

Change for the worse

A manager is offering a pay rise to his lovely and young secretary.

"Here's the deal," he says. "I'm going to drop £50 on the floor. If you can pick it up before I do anything, you keep the money."

The girl thinks about it, having no doubt as to what this 'before I do anything' means. But, then again, the manager's not a young man any more and he's certainly not as fast and supple as her.

"I'll come back to you tomorrow on that one," she replies.

Back home, she phones a friend of hers and explains the situation to him.

The friend drops a £50 note on the floor. The girl has picked it up before he even starts unzipping. They repeat the simulation a few times and in the end the secretary feels confident she can grab the £50 note before the old codger of a manager can get his trousers down.

Her friend wishes her good luck and the following day she's off to work. He sees her come back at lunchtime, bow-legged and her hair undone.

"What happened?" he asks.

"I had no idea he was going to drop £50 in £1 coins," she replies tiredly.

The birds and the bees

A little girl walks up to her dad and asks him: "Dad, what's sex?"

The dad sighs and takes his head in his hands. Knowing it had to happen one day doesn't make it any easier. After inhaling deeply, he sets out to explain what sex is. He starts with the birds and the bees, the pollination process, then passes on to eggs, sperm, puberty, menstruation, wet dreams, hormones, the lot. Seeing his daughter's rapt expression, he thinks: "Hell, might

FHM *PRESENTS ...*

as well go all the way", so he starts talking about masturbation, sexual intercourse, the Kama Sutra, bestiality, bondage, sodomy, rape, sex toys, the G-spot: in short he talks for a good hour about sex and all sorts of sex-related subjects. His daughter is still riveted to his every word.

"Why did you want to know about sex, anyway?" he asks her.

"Eh? Oh, mum said dinner would be ready in a couple of sex. I guess it's cold now,"

Filthy lucre

A bloke enters a bank and says to the lady behind the counter: "I'd like to open a fucking account with your shitty bank."

"I'm sorry?" the woman behind the counter says.

"I said I wanted to open a fucking account in your shitty bank. Hard of hearing, you stupid bitch?"

The woman is incensed. "Please vacate the premises, sir," she orders the offensive customer.

"Oh, fuck off. Get your fingers out of your fat arse and get me the manager."

The woman turns around quickly and gets her manager.

"What seems to be the problem there?" the manager asks, ready to call the police.

"I said to your stupid bitch of a clerk that I wanted to open a fucking account. I'm here on holiday and I need to transfer three million fucking pounds for a couple of weeks."

"And this piece of shit is giving you grief?"

Feeling fruity

It's the summer holidays and the regular sales assistant at the local bakery is off to Barbados for a week. The baker has to hire a new girl, a youngster with a penchant for short skirts.

A guy come into the bakery and has a look at the different kinds of bread available. He decides on the raisin bread and is quite surprised to see the young woman start climbing a short ladder to reach the bread on the last shelf. He's also quite surprised by the view her short skirt is giving him, and decides on the spot that raisin bread is going to be a major part of his daily diet from now on.

After a few days, words of the mini-skirted young woman has spread all over town and males queue up to order raisin bread. Fed up with the whole process of climbing up and down the ladder, the lass vents her irritation on one old codger.

"So, is yours raisin too?" she asks, her fists on her hips.

"Nope," croaks the old man, "but it's startin' to twitch."

No comebacks

This employee is incredibly bored at work and the holidays are still a good week away. His stress levels are sky-high and he decides that it is actually a matter of mental health to have a laugh, right now. He dials an extension at random and says: "Hey, arsehole, move your arse and bring me a coffee, will you?"

There's a silence at the other end of the line; then a man replies: "Do you have any idea who you're talking to, fartbrain?"

"Nope."

"I'm the general manager of the company that used to have the misfortune of having employed you."

"Is that so? And do you know who you're talking to?"
"No."
"Well, that's a relief," says the guy, hanging up.

CHAPTER FOUR
Jokes for Hotels

Magic fingers

The hotel manager is in a huff: the piano player has eloped with a beautiful heiress again and he urgently needs someone to replace him. He places an advert in the papers, auditions a few, but none is suave or competent enough. Desperate, he's wringing his hands at the door of the restaurant when he's interrupted in his righteous bout of self-pity by a bum.

"Go away," he shouts, quite happy to have someone to vent his frustration on.

"Come on, give me a break. I'm a piano player – honest," says the smelly one, pointing at the notice stuck to the door. "You're looking for someone; I'm your man."

"You must be joking!"

"Come on, man, just hear me play."

Desperate, the hotel manager agrees. He escorts the bum to the piano, puts some newspaper on the stool, inspects the bum's hands for signs of long nails or greasy marks and, satisfied that the guy's hands are not too dirty, lets him play.

The bum is a genius. The melodies he extracts from the instrument are pure, delicate and out of this world.

"That was very good," the hotel manager nods. "What's it called?"

"Oh, it's a little piece I wrote called 'The day I cooked lasagne and burnt it in the oven.'"

"Er, yes. Quite unusual. You know anything else?"

"Sure," the bum replies. He launches into in a rather funky number, both melodious and snazzy. The hotel manager is bowled over.

"This is great music!" he exclaims. "You wrote that, too?"

"Yeah; it's called 'The day I rode her like a beast across the bed from behind.'"

"I see," the hotel manager says. "Listen: you got the job – only don't answer if people ask you the titles of your pieces, OK? They're just too weird."

The bum agrees with a shrug and is taken to the laundry, where he's supposed to find a tux for the evening. Unfortunately, the only suit available is three sizes too small for him. Nonetheless, as it's too late to go and buy one that fits, he is forced into it by the manager – after a long bath, a manicure and a haircut – and then ushered to the piano.

The bum is magnificent. His playing is masterly and he holds his audience enthralled. The hotel manager rubs his hands together as the piano-playing entices the couples to romance – and buy champagne. After a few numbers, a hot-looking bird approaches the bum and tells him in a husky voice: "You play pretty well; do you know you have a hairy butt and your balls are falling out of your pants but I like that in a man?"

At this, the bum smiles beatifically and says: "Do I know it? I wrote it!"

If music be the food of love

The appeal of the anonymity of a hotel room has made a husband quite raunchy and he tells his wife: "Darling, I'm gonna play you like a violin."

To which she replies coyly: "Actually, I'd rather have you play me like a harmonica."

In case of emergency

A musician carrying a big case is booking in at the hotel desk. The receptionist, none too bright, asks him what the big case is for.

"It's a viola," he replies. "It's a musical instrument, a bit like a violin, but bigger."

"I like the violin," the girl says, picking up his credit card.

"Well, I used to play the violin, but now I play the viola," the musician explains.

"Why did you change?"

"The viola holds more beer," he replies.

His hand in marriage

This older man has married a frisky little number, much younger than him. They decide to celebrate the event with a weekend by the sea. They book into the hotel and the young bride climbs on to the bed straight away, ready for some action. Unfortunately, the hubby's feeling a bit under the weather.

"So, are we going to have rampant sex together?" the horny young bride asks mischievously.

The husband holds out his hand. The wife counts the fingers.

"Five times?" she squeals in delight.

"No; that means, 'Pick a finger.'"

There's just one little thing outstanding...

A newlywed couple are sitting by the pool, having a rest after the ceremony and getting ready for the night to come. The wife, stretched out on a reclining chair, takes of her husband's hand and says: "Honey, we're married now, so I can finally tell you my secret; I've never seen a penis before."

The husband's quite surprised but also quite excited, so he forgets about the pool and the rest and rushes his wife to the bedroom, where he swiftly pulls his pants down.

"This is a penis," he tells her.

"Oh, I see," the bride exclaims. "It's like a cock, only smaller."

'Til death do us part

Two men are sitting at neighbouring tables in a hotel bar. After a short while they strike up a conversation and, after talking about the weather and the football results, they start on women.

"I'm married to a lovely blonde," says one. "We're very much in love. You married?"

"No, I'm afraid not," the other replies.

"Ah, that's too bad: but then again, I gather unmarried men live longer than married men."

"Nah, I don't think they actually do. It just feels that way."

Role reversal

"What if we tried a new position tonight, Honey?" the hubby asks his wife. "Come on, we're on holiday, let's experiment."

"Sure," the wife replies. "Tell you what; you go and lie down and I'll stay on the sofa watching TV and farting."

Scarred for life

A couple are about to have sex for the first time. They've been
dating for some time now but haven't got any further than a chaste
goodnight kiss. Tonight, the girl has decided to take matters into
her own hands, so to speak, and is taking the bloke home with her.
They have some fun on the sofa until, unable to wait any longer,
she drags the guy to her bedroom. He is strangely reluctant, and gets
undressed with painful slowness. When he pulls his trousers down,
the woman discovers his knees are all spotty and knobbly.

"What happened to you? Did you have an accident or
something?"

"No, nothing like that," the guy replies. "I had kneesles when I
was young."

"You had what?"

"Kneesles."

"Knessles? You're pulling my leg, right? You mean measles," the
girl says with a laugh.

"No, not measles: kneesles. It a very rare condition."

The girl shrugs and helps him out of his socks. To her surprise,
she notices that his toes are weirdly shaped.

"Tolio," the guy explains.

"Tolio? You mean polio."

"No, it's another pretty rare condition. It's not polio."

The girl shakes her head but, after all, she's not really interested in
his toes. She grabs his pants and pulls. There is a moment of silence.

"OK; don't tell me: smallcox, right?"

It's a miracle

A couple have been together for quite some time now and their
relationship has seen better days. Today, the husband is sitting at the

bar of the hotel watching the young beauties go by while his wife complains about the price of her martini.

Following her husband's gaze, she stops and remarks, "I wish I had bigger tits." To which the husband answers: "No problem. All you have to do is to rub toilet paper all over them."

"Toilet paper? Why on earth should I rub toilet paper over my breasts? How's that going to make them grow bigger?"

"Why not?" he asks. "It worked for your arse."

The gender gap

A young couple have been together for a short time and are very much in love. Everything they do is perfect, and they find amusement and wonder in the simplest things.

One morning, the woman wakes up and finds her lover lost in the contemplation of her face, something she finds rather sweet.

"You're so beautiful in the morning when you wake up," the bloke says adoringly. "The way you rub your eyes is so touching."

"I only do that because I don't have any balls to scratch," the girl replies.

Best left unsaid

Three couples find themselves in adjacent rooms in a hotel. As they are getting undressed, the first man says to his wife, "What a big arse you have," so she throws him out into the corridor. The second man says to his wife, "What big tits you have," and is likewise flung out of the room. The two men are soon joined by a third. "Did you put your foot in it too?" the second asks him. "No," he replies, "but I could have!"

The secret of a happy marriage

Two girls are having a last holiday together. One of them is getting married and they just want to celebrate her carefree single life for a little while longer.

"This is the last bit of fun you'll ever have," her friend tells the bride-to-be.

"Oh, come on!" she laughs.

"Just take this bit of advice," her friend continues. "Right from the beginning, tell him that you need to have at least one night a week out with the girls."

The bride-to-be nods.

"And then don't waste your time on the girls," the other finishes, draining her glass.

Colour me stupid

A hotel manager is talking to his contractor about what colour to repaint the rooms.

"I'd like a little bit of a change," he says. "This time, let's have the suites pale ochre and the ordinary rooms pale blue."

"Sure," the contractor says. He writes this down in his notebook, then walks to the window and yells: "Green side up!"

The manager is somewhat surprised, but he doesn't want to be distracted from the task in hand and carries on: "You'll need to check the plumbing as well; we've had a couple of complaints this year, might as well tackle that straight from the start."

"Right you are," the contractor says, putting everything down in his notebook. Then he taps the pencil on the page, again walks to the window and yells: "Green side up!"

"What is the matter?" the manager asks. "Why do you keep yelling that out of the window?"

"I'm sorry," the contractor replies. "It's just that the crew I hired to lay the turf in the garden are all blondes."

Is the right answer!

The manager of a posh hotel is looking for a receptionist. The girl doesn't need to be too well-versed in booking methods, as training is provided, but she needs to be pretty, smart and friendly.

Such a young lady is sitting in front of him right now, but she's quite nervous. In an attempt at breaking the ice, he asks her: "Now, if you could have a chat with anyone, alive or dead, who would it be?"

The poor girl looks at him with wide, panicky eyes, thinks for a moment and replies: "Well, I'd pick up the live one, I guess."

That's a date

A busload of college kids has just invaded the hotel lobby and the place is suddenly cramped. A man is struggling with his suitcase and, while trying to negotiate his exit from the lift, he bumps into a woman. He is mortified, but at the same time aroused by the firmness of this woman's breast, which he can't help but feel through her dress. He apologises to her with an embarrassed smile.

"Madam, if your heart is as soft as your breast, I know you'll forgive me," he says to her.

"Sir," she replies roguishly, "if your cock's as hard as your elbow, I'm in room 221."

Freeze a jolly good fellow

"I'm on holiday with my wife," a husband tells the hotel barman, "and tonight" – raising his glass in a mock toast – "I'm celebrating my ice anniversary."

"Ice anniversary? I've never heard of that one."

"It's seven years. That's how long we've been married, and that's how long my wife's been serving me frozen meals."

Do not disturb

A woman is on holiday on her own. She's renting a room in a nice, friendly hotel. As she's a very warm and polite person, she quickly becomes the favourite of all the staff, who have to contend with all sorts of people. She spends a whole week in the hotel and the staff can't fail to notice that her face is becoming more drawn, her complexion paler and her expression sadder. The director of the hotel comes over to her table one evening and sits down next to her.

"Forgive my presumption," he begins, "but we've noticed that you don't seem as happy as when you first arrived here. Is anything the matter?"

"Oh, it has nothing to do with your hotel, let me assure you." she says. "Everybody's so nice and the room's lovely. Unfortunately, I'm plagued by these weird nightmares. I keep dreaming there's a man under my bed who's going to leap out and murder me."

"I see," says the manager. "I know a psychiatrist who may be able to help; we see all sorts of people here and I've done business with him a few times. He seems to be quite efficient and honest."

The woman thanks him and, the following day goes to see this psychiatrist.

"It all has to do with your childhood," he tells her. "Come and see me once a week for at least six months. I charge £100 a session."

The woman thanks him, but says she can't really afford the treatment. Back at the hotel, she tells the manager how it went and how she'll just have to live with her dusturbing dreams. The manager strokes his chin for a while, pondering, and then whispers something to her.

The following day the woman comes downstairs in much better form. She is radiant and obviously happy, and seeks out the manager so she can shake his hand.

"It worked. What a brilliant idea!"

"Simple, really," the manager says. "I was sure you'd sleep better if we sawed off the legs of the bed."

Nun fun

A couple of businessmen have booked two hotel rooms and are refreshing themselves before an evening meeting. The first guy steps into the shower and realises that there is no soap. Not bothering to dress, he quickly runs next door to borrow a couple of bars. Back in the corridor, he spots three nuns walking towards him and, panicking, decides simply to freeze and pretend he's a statue.

The nuns walk by and his ruse seems to be working when the last one stops and points at him.

"This is a very nicely crafted statue," she says. Mischievously, she pulls on the businessman's penis. The guy drops one of the soaps he's been holding, managing nonetheless to remain silent.

"Look; a soap dispenser," the nun squeaks. Her friends stop and turn around to have a look. Another nun has a go at penis-pulling and, sure enough, another bar of soap drops on the carpet. The third nun grabs the penis in her turn, pulls it once, twice, three times and nothing happens. Undeterred, she carries on pulling and pushing on the thing and suddenly exclaims: "How cool is that? Hand cream!"

The human condition

A customer is asking for directions at the hotel information desk when a tired-looking bloke comes down the stairs. He shuffles to the counter, drops his keys and slowly leaves.

"What's the matter with him?" the customer asks.

"He's an agnostic, a dyslexic and an insomniac all rolled into one," the clerk answers with a pitying shake of his head. "He stays awake all night wondering if there really is a dog."

Sticky end

The hotel is in shambles: a body has been found in room 101. The maid has discovered a man covered in chocolate ice cream, with a flake up each nostril, smeared with strawberry sauce and with hundreds and thousands sprinkled all over him. The detective strokes his chin, nods and says: "Looks like he topped himself."

It sticks in your head

A guy walks into a hotel bar and orders twelve whiskies. The barman serves him and watches the bloke drink one shot after another.

"Celebrating something, friend?" he asks.

"Yeah: my first blow job ever," the guy replies.

The barman's face lights up. "Way to go, man. Now *that* is something worth celebrating. Let me get you one on the house!"

"Nah; thanks anyway," the bloke says, "but if 12 whiskies won't take the taste away, I doubt another one'll make any difference."

Sorted

A deaf couple are spending their honeymoon in a posh hotel in Majorca. They're very much in love but, because of their disability, they can't really communicate at night, when the light's out. After a disappointing first night spent fumbling about, the wife comes up with a solution. Using sign language at breakfast, she says: "If you want to make love to me at night, grab my left breast. If you *don't* want to, grab the right breast."

The husband nods and signs: "Good idea, honey. We'll do the same for me. If you want to make love to me, pull on my penis once. If you *don't*, pull on my penis 50 times."

Politeness costs nothing

A newlywed couple are having a mild disagreement during their first night together. The bride, it appears, is a bit of a stickler for niceties and politeness and doesn't really appreciate her new husband's thinly-veiled sexual advances.

"I expect proper manners in bed," she declares, "just as I do at the dinner table. We're not animals and we should behave like civilized people."

Annoyed by his wife's formality, the groom nods soberly, takes a deep breath and wordlessly gets into bed.

"Is that better?" he asks.

"Yes," replies the wife, getting into bed next to him.

"Very good, darling," the husband whispered. "Now would you be so kind as to pass me your tits?"

Reet petite

An American is staying in a hotel in Paris. He's been pissing off the staff for a week by complaining about how small things are here, compared to America. The Eiffel Tower, the Louvres, the Chateau de Versailles; everything's tiny compared to the buildings back home. After a week of being slagged off, the staff have had enough and decide to pay him back before he leaves. To this effect, a maid surreptitiously places a lobster in the guy's bed.

At the end of the day, just as the American's about to get into bed (which is, of course, much smaller than an American bed), a heart-stopping shout rings out. He rushes out of his room and grabs the maid in terror.

"There's a huge... Oh, my God it's all red and enormous!" he stutters.

"Ah, yes," the maid says mischievously. "It's so difficult to get rid of bedbugs. They're always coming back whatever we do."

Outstanding qualities

A hotel manager is looking for a new receptionist. Three young women reply to the add. The manager decides to each them the same question and to compare the results.

"Let's imagine that you find a £50 note in front of your desk. What do you do?"

"I put a notice on the counter and try to find out who lost it," says the first.

"I put it in the safe. If the note's not claimed after a month, I keep it," the second says.

"I give it straight away to a security guard," says the third.

Who gets the job?

Answer: the one with the nicest tits.

Parting of the ways

A couple are in bed in a hotel in France. The woman puts down her book and exclaims: "Now that *is* interesting!"

"What is, dear?" her husband asks.

"According to this book, if a man loses his hair at the back, it means he's a great thinker. If he loses his hair at the front, he's a great lover."

The husband, disconsolately, passes a hand in his luxuriant hair.

"So what does it mean when you're *not* losing your hair?"

"It means you think you're a great lover."

This isn't working out

A couple are having a drink in a hotel bar. Although they're in Copacabana, supposedly on holiday, they still manage to find something to argue about.

"We've been together six years and I don't remember us agreeing on anything," the husband complains.

"You're wrong. We've been together seven years."

CHAPTER FIVE
Nightclub Jokes

A date with destiny

A guy is sitting on his own at the bar of a nightclub, hoping to score at least once during his holidays. Lo and behold, as if a higher being was actually listening to his inner thoughts, a magnificent blonde walks in and sits down next to him.

As is often the case, there's quite a gap between dreams and reality and, although this guy's been rehearsing chat-up lines all his life, now the time has come to actually come up with a witty introduction, he finds himself tongue-tied.

"Come on," he admonishes himself. "Look, she's beautiful, she's alone, she came to sit right next to you; now's your chance."

A few times he takes a deep breath, on the verge of facing the blonde and saying something, but every time he hesitates and blushes and points his face back into his glass. After a few minutes, the girl gets off her stool and walks away.

"You've blown it, you stupid sod; she's gone now and you didn't find the courage to do anything. You're pathetic," the guy castigates himself. He orders another drink, resolving to drown his sorrows, when the blonde comes back and sits next to him again, flashing him a lovely smile. "This is it!" the guy thinks. "This is a sign from destiny. I've got to do something. I've got to stop hesitating and say the first thing that comes into my mind. It'll be fine." He turns to face the girl and says: "Been for a shit, then, eh?"

No fool like an old fool

An old geezer's sitting at the bar in a very trendy nightclub. He's come in with a pretty brunette, who since then has deserted him and is now dancing very close to a very handsome and muscular hunk.

The old man sighs, turns to the bartender and says: "I've been working hard all my life. I've been saving all my money for years and years." He points forlornly to the brunette on the dancefloor. "Now I can finally afford to buy stuff that only the young can enjoy."

Too much information

A young woman comes back from holiday and confronts her mum with some news.

"Mum, I'm pregnant."

"Oh, Sally... How could you let this happen? Where was your head at?"

"Against the windscreen."

Irresistible force

A barman is squeezing lemons for a cocktail he's invented. A customer's watching him at work and says: "Don't throw away this lemon; I'm sure I can squeeze some more from it."

The barman laughs and hands the skins over. Sure enough, the bloke manages to squeeze half a glass of lemon juice from them.

"Now, that's a neat trick, man," the barman says, clearly impressed.

"There's no trick," the bloke says. "I'm a tax inspector."

Polished performance

A bloke has a special pair of shoes which are extremely well polished. Of course, he wears them in clubs and uses a special pick-up line. It goes a bit like this: he dances with a bird, takes on a mysterious air, tells her he's psychic and, as proof, tells her the colour of her knickers, which he can see reflected in his shiny shoes. This isn't to everyone's taste, but it works more often than not, and it's done the trick with this particular young woman, who goes back to her friend and says: "I met this psychic guy last night; he could tell me the colour of my knickers just by looking deep into my eyes!"

"That's bullshit," her friend says. "Introduce me; I want to have a good look at this bloke."

The following night, the friend is introduced to the mystical knicker-reader, who describes accurately the colour of the girl's panties. The girl is astonished since, as far as she can see, he hasn't cheated and she's been careful not to put herself in any panty-showing situations.

"You know what?" says another friend the following night, "I'll dance with this guy. I don't wear any knickers, so we'll see what he's got to say about it."

True to her word, the third friend dances with the psychic bloke without wearing any panties. The guy's face is flushed throughout the dance and he doesn't go through his psychic routine with her.

"Is there anything wrong?" the girl asks with a smile.

"No, no; it's nothing."

"I know," she says, lightly touching his arm. "It's because I'm not wearing any panties, right?"

The bloke looks at her and sighs in relief. "So that's what it is! I though my shoes had a crack in them!"

All clever stuff

A guy's sitting at the bar in a trendy nightclub. He's been trying unsuccessfully to score, but hasn't had much luck. Another bloke next to him has noticed his lack of success.

"What you need is some serious marketing techniques," he says. "I work in marketing myself; I know how it's done."

"Oh, yeah?" the bloke asks, not very happy at his sexual failure being so obvious.

"Absolutely," his new friend continues. "You see, if you walk up to a bird and say: "I'm terrific in bed", that's called direct marketing. If you ask a friend to go and tell her you're terrific in bed, that's called advertising. Now, let's say you've met a girl and she agrees to give you her phone number when you part. If you phone her up later on and say you're terrific in bed, it's called telemarketing."

"I see," the other bloke says. "That makes sense."

"If you meet her again the following week and ask her if she remembers how terrific you were, it's called customer relationship management. Now, imagine you meet another bird. You tuck yourself in, you quickly brush your hair, open the door to her when she leaves and light her cigarette while saying that you're terrific in bed; that's called public relations. If a bird walks up to you and says she's heard you're terrific in bed, it's brand awareness."

"Well, how come you're on your own tonight if you know so much about it?" the guy asks.

"Well, if you go out to a nightclub, spot a bird who's super-fit and talk about her with a stranger, and then do nothing about it but get shit-faced, it's called the reality of the market."

Birthday suit

The fancy dress party is a success. The guests include Marilyn, Peter Pan, a few hobbits and a young woman who is naked except for a pair of black leather gloves and a pair of black leather knee-high boots.

A guest notices her and, puzzled, walks over to her. "What are you dressed up as?" he asks her.

"Can't you guess?" she says. "I'm the five of spades."

Mucky talk

Two condoms on holiday walk past a gay bar. One says to the other: "Hey, do you fancy dropping in there and getting shit-faced?"

If you can't beat them...

A farmer's son is out on the town and ends up in a night club, sitting at the bar and nursing a beer. He spots a couple of stunning birds at the far end, turns to the bartender and says: "Give these two lasses a drink on me."

The barman shrugs, turns around to prepare the drinks, but hesitates. "Listen mate; if you think you're going to score, I've got to tell you that you don't stand a chance."

"Who says?" the bloke asks, ready to take offence.

"Well, they won't be interested; they're lesbians."

"Lesbians? What's that? Is it contagious?"

The barman stares at the farmer's son, shrugs and replies: "Go and ask them, mate. That's the best way to learn."

The bloke thinks that's fair enough and walks up to the two birds.

"The barman's been telling me you're lesbians," he says to them. "What's a lesbian? You look healthy enough to me."

They both fall into a fit of the giggles. Finally, still hiccupping, one of them replies: "Well, being a lesbian means we like kissing girls. We like caressing them, we like touching them and licking them."

The bloke stares at them and a grin slowly spreads across his face. "Barman," he shouts, turning around, "Three beers for us lesbians!"

A taste of the country

Two blokes are on holiday in Spain and decide to have a look at what the local clubs have on offer. They choose a club at random and take a seat by the bar. The place is teeming with birds of all styles and the two blokes are duly impressed.

Soon one spots a charming brunette wearing a mini-skirt which leaves nothing to the imagination. He nudges his mate and orders an extra drink, carries it over to her and soon they're chatting away like old friends. Fifteen minutes later, they get up and walk out of the club. In passing, the bloke gives his friend a conspiratorial wink. Sure enough, some time later, the bloke comes back and confesses to his friend that he's been out for a quick shag. "Look," he says, pointing her out to his friend. "She's back sitting where she was when I pulled her. I tell you, she's really up for it. Why don't you go and have a go?"

The friend thinks it over, shrugs and approaches the girl. They chat for a few minutes and, sure enough, it's his turn to go out and sample some Spanish hospitality.

When he comes back, his friend's waiting for him with a beer.

"Cool holiday, eh? Mind you, she wasn't that good. I think my wife's better at blow-jobs."

"Definitely," his friend agrees.

Don't get involved

A guy's off to the toilet after a solid hour of dancing. He's just finished when a bloke without hands comes in. He stands in front of the urinals but has obvious problems with his zip.

"Need a hand?" the first bloke asks, feeling he ought to be a Good Samaritan.

"Well, if you could undo my zip and pull my pecker out for me, that'd be great."

The guy pulls the bloke's zip down and is confronted by a horrible-looking dick, all covered in pus, angry red spots and yellowish veins. He recoils, but a promise is a promise, so he gingerly pulls the guy's shlong out. The guy pisses a long stream of blood-streaked urine and, with a nod, asks for the zip to be pulled back up again.

The guy complies, but asks: "I couldn't help noticing; what's wrong with your penis?"

The bloke takes his hands out of his pockets and says: "I haven't the faintest, but I sure ain't touching it."

Do not engage mouth before brain is in gear

Three women met around the swimming pool in the resort's best hotel a week ago and have become firm friends. They're having a girls' night out and are sitting at a table with a few drinks, discussing their respective blokes.

"When I suck Pete's cock, his balls are always very cold," one of them says.

"Yeah, Mike's the same," agrees another. "It can put me off sometimes. What about John?"

"I don't know," the last woman replies, blushing crimson. "We don't do that."

"Why not?" the others laugh.

"Well, I don't know..." she says lamely.

"Try it. A great blow-job's the best way to keep your man," the first woman tells her wisely.

The following day they meet again by the poolside. The third woman sports an ugly black eye.

"What happened to you?" the others ask, horrified. "Did John do that to you?"

"Yeah; well, I went down on him last night, like you said," she explains, "and then I said it was strange that his balls felt so warm compared to how cold Pete's and Mike's were..."

That'll teach her

A bloke walks into a nightclub in the south of France and sits at the bar. He's not scored once in a whole week, so he decides to talk to the girl sitting next to him.

"Would you like to dance?" he asks in his most charming voice.

The girl looks him up and down in the way she'd inspect a particularly nasty insect.

"I don't like to dance," she replies haughtily, "and if I did, I don't think I'd like to dance with you." She then returns her attention to her drink.

The bloke, seriously pissed off, taps her on the shoulder and says: "I'm sorry, I don't think you quite understood me. I said your arse looked fat in that sloppy skirt."

Ready for action

Two friends are getting ready to go to the club one evening. One of them dresses quite scantily and her friend can't help but notice.

"Wow; you're on the pull tonight, aren't you?"

Her friend says nothing, but winks at her suggestively.

"And you're not wearing any knickers!"

"Well, when you go to a concert, you don't wear earplugs, do you?"

CHAPTER SIX

Restaurant Jokes

Amphibious assault

An American couple are in a restaurant in Paris. They're feeling brave and order the frogs' legs, but now they've got this plate of chicken-like sticks in front of them, they don't quite know what to do with them. The wife is inclined to just dip in and get her fingers greasy, but she's not quite sure; after all, who knows how these weird Frenchmen eat these things?

Hesitant, she finally hails a waiter: "I'm sorry," she says in a small but piercing voice. "Is it OK to eat frogs' legs with your fingers?"

The waiter looks at her for a moment and replies: "Not really, madam. You usually eat your fingers separately."

Lovely grub

On holiday in India, little Johnny asks: "Daddy, are caterpillars good to eat?" His father is irritated. "I've told you not to talk about things like that during meals." "Why did you want to know?" asks his mother. Johnny says: "I saw one on daddy's lettuce, but it's gone now."

Having a ball

A tourist goes to a restaurant in Madrid and orders the dish of the day. When his dinner arrives, it consists of two rubbery-looking balls of greyish meat in some sort of gravy.

"What is it?" he asks curiously.

"This is a very famous Spanish delicacy. It's called cojones. It means balls: testicles. These are the testicles of the bull that fought today in the ring."

The customer blanches at that. Unfortunately, the waiter seems to be very proud of having served this to him and the man can't get away from eating it. He gulps, plays for a while with the meat ball floating in the gravy, closes his eyes and takes a bite. To his enormous surprise, it is quite delicious. It's so good, in fact, that the following evening he orders the same thing. This time, though, the balls in his plate are quite noticeably smaller than the ones he had the previous night. He calls the waiter and asks for an explanation: "Tell me; these cojones seem to be much smaller tonight than last night. How come?"

"Ah, si, Señor," the waiter replies with a bow. "You see, the bull doesn't always lose."

It's all geek to me

A geek is visiting Silicon Valley and is eating in a big geek's hangout.

"Sorry, but there seems to be a fly in my soup," he says to the waiter.

"I can't see any fly, sir. Are you sure?"

"I'm positive, yes; there's a fly in my soup."

"Mmmmm... try it again. The fly might have gone."

"Er, no; it's still there."

"I see. May I enquire what you are using your soup with?"

"Er... a soup spoon?"

"Strange; this should be working, then. Have you tried using something else to eat your soup, like a fork?"

"I doubt a fork would make the fly in my soup disappear."

"What version of the soup are you eating, sir?"

"Version? You mean flavour? I'm having the soup of the day. It's tomato soup."

"Ah, I see now, sir. You need to upgrade to the latest soup."

"You mean you have more than one soup of the day per day?"

"The soup of the day changes every hour, sir."

"Oh. I see. And what is the flavour of the latest soup?"

"Potato and leek, sir."

"OK, give me a bowl of potato and leek soup then."

The waiter arrives a few minutes later with a bowl of mushroom soup and the bill.

"Mushroom soup? What happened to potato and leek?"

"I'm sorry; it wasn't quite ready yet, sir."

"Oh, OK then."

On the bill is itemised: "Soup of the day: $5.00. Upgrade to soup of the day: $5.00. Call fee to customer service: $150."

Eastern wisdom

A man walks into a Chinese restaurant but is told that there will be at least a 20-minute wait and is asked if he'd like to wait in the bar. He goes into the bar and the bartender says, "What'll it be?" The man replies, "Give me a Stoli with a twist." The bartender squints at him for a few seconds, then smiles and says: "Once upon a time there were four little pigs..."

Pet sounds

An Australian backpacker is stranded is Asia. Flat broke, he decides to look for a little job, so that he can get enough money to eat and think about his next step. He finds employment in a local restaurant. One day the owner asks him to go to the shop for a couple of tins of cat food.

"Good morning; I'd like two tins of cat food, please."

"Aren't you the Australian working in the Chinese restaurant?"

"Why, yes."

"I won't sell you any cat food. It's to put in your spring rolls, isn't it?"

"No, not at all: The owner's got two cats; it's for them!"

The shop owner is adamant: if he wants any cat food, he's got to show him the cats. The Australian guy shrugs, goes back to the restaurant, picks up the cats and shows them to the shopkeeper. Still suspicious, he sells him a couple of tins of cat food. Some time passes and the Australian is asked to go to the shop again to get a couple of tins of dog food.

"No! I gave in last time, but there's no way I'm selling you dog food. Cats don't eat dog food!"

"The boss has got two cats *and* two dogs. That's why I want dog food. It's not for the cats."

"I don't believe you," the shop owner says. "Show me the dogs."

The Australian backpacker sighs, walks back to the restaurant, picks up the dogs and shows them to the grocer, who reluctantly sells him some dog food. A week passes and the shop owner see the bloke come back with a bucket full of something that really stinks. "What do you want?" he asks the young man, wrinkling his nose.

"I need a pack of loo rolls for the restaurant. I know you don't trust me, so I just brought the proof with me; saves me going back again."

Manners maketh mean

One day, Juan and Jose go to a Spanish restaurant for dinner. As soon as the waiter brings out two steaks, Juan quickly picks out the bigger one for himself. Jose isn't happy about that, and demands: "When are you going to learn to be polite?"

Juan replies: "If you had the chance to pick first, which one would you pick?"

"The smaller piece, of course."

"What are you grumbling about, then?"

Air con

A customer is bothering the waiter in a French restaurant. First, he asks for the air conditioning to be turned up because he's too hot; then he wants it turned down because he's too cold, and so on for about half an hour. Surprisingly, the waiter is very patient. He walks back and forth and never once gets angry. Finally, a second customer asks him why he didn't throw out the pest. "Oh, I don't care," says the waiter with a smile. "We don't even have an air conditioner."

Nuts to you

A guy in Australia goes to visit his aunt in a nursing home. It turns out it's her nap time. The bloke's got nothing to do, the Outback isn't especially appealing and so he just sits down in a chair in her room, flips through a few magazines and munches on some peanuts sitting in a bowl on the table. Eventually the aunt wakes up and her nephew realises he's absent-mindedly finished the entire bowl of peanuts.

"I'm so sorry, Auntie, I've eaten all your peanuts!"

"Jeez, that's OK, Duncan," the aunt replied. "After I've sucked the chocolate off, I don't much care for them anyway."

Dirty dealings

Two rather arrogant American guys are sitting in a tea shop in Shrewsbury, Shropshire. The waiter approaches and asks them what they'd like to order.

"I'll go native and have tea," says one Yank with a wink to his friend.

"If you can do it, so can I," says his mate. "Tea for me, too – and make sure the cup's clean."

The waiter gives them an entirely false smile and returns shortly afterwards. He puts the tray on the table and says: "Two teas. Now then: which of you asked for the clean cup?"

From here to eternity

Two Italian violinists are best friends. They went to music school together, they had their first contracts in the same orchestra: in short, they've always been around for one another. As old age is creeping up on them, they make a pact that whoever dies first will contact the other and tell him what life in heaven is like.

Poor Roberto has a heart attack and dies. He manages to make contact with Antonio the next day and, via the ouija board, Antonio asks him what life's like in Heaven. Roberto replies: "Well, it's great, but I've got good news, and then I've got bad news. The good news is that there's a fantastic orchestra up here, and in fact, we're playing Scheherazade, your favourite piece, tomorrow night."

"So what's the bad news?"

"Well, you're booked to play the solo."

Waiter, waiter!

"Here, waiter, my plate's wet!"
  "That's the soup, sir!"

"Here, waiter, there's no chicken in this chicken pie."
  "So what? You don't get dog in a dog biscuit, do you?"

"Here, waiter, what's the meaning of this fly in my tea cup?"
  "I wouldn't know, sir. I'm a waiter, not a fortune-teller."

"Here, waiter, this egg tastes rather strong."
  "Never mind, sir; the tea's nice and weak."

"Here, waiter, does the pianist play requests?"
  "Yes, sir."
  "Then ask him to play tiddlywinks 'til I've finished my meal."

CHAPTER SEVEN

Sports Jokes

Master baiters

A priest is taking his morning stroll on the beach in Sydney when he sees a couple of guys dragging the body of a third guy out of the water by a rope. "That's what I like to see:" the priest reflects aloud, smiling. "A man helping his fellow-man.".

"Well," one guy mutters to the other, "you can tell that bloke hasn't got a clue about shark-fishing..."

Teed off

His missus has gone shopping, his little boy's bored with the swimming pool, so Dad has no option but to take his son golfing with him. He's quite relieved, however, to learn that there's a kids' learning session on today. He signs the lad in for the morning and heads off to the first tee.

"OK," the instructor says to the boy. "You see the little flag over there? I'm going to ask you to swing this ball as close to the flag as possible." He holds up a golf ball, puts it on the tee, passes the kid a club and encourages him to have a go.

The little boy squints at the flag, weighs his club and gives the ball a solid whack. They walk to the green and, to the instructor's amazement, he realises that the ball has ended up a mere five centimetres from the hole.

"That's very good, sonny," he congratulates the boy. "Now, the overall aim of golf is to put this ball in the hole."

"What?" the little boy exclaims, indignant. "Why didn't you say so in the first place?"

Hang on in there

A couple have booked a rock-climbing weekend and find themselves at the bottom of an impressive cliff face. Their instructor is there, tying people together with thick ropes. When their turn comes, the husband tries to lighten the mood by saying: "Hey, why are you tying us up like that? Afraid we'll get lost?"

"Oh no," the instructor replies. "It's just to prevent the sensible ones trying to go home half-way up."

Simple answer

A mountain guide has a walker from hell on his day tour. It's a middle-aged tourist who just won't shut up. After having answered at least a hundred silly questions, the guide's had enough.

"This is spectacular," the tourist says. "Tell me: how did these rocks get there?"

"They were brought there by a glacier," the guide replies, grinding his teeth.

"I don't see any glacier."

"Oh my! Maybe it's gone back for more rocks."

Sent to the bottom

A man has been enjoying skiing all week, but now's the time to have some harmless, old-fashioned fun and go back to his roots. It's 8pm. He picks up his old skates and heads over to the pond. Being the dead of winter, he knows the pond's frozen solid and quite safe to skate on. He sits down on a bench and is putting his skates on when he hears some muffled shouts coming from the pond. Quietly, he skates to the far bank and, to his enormous surprise, finds a couple having a go at evening outdoor sex on the ice. The shapes across the pond are clearly those of a busty woman enthusiastically riding a fat guy on the ice. They seem to be having a great time when suddenly, maybe due to body heat or friction, the ice starts to make alarming sounds. The busy couple, wrapped up in their nocturnal exercise, don't hear anything and just carry on until, with a mighty ripping sound, the ice yawns open under the guy. The woman, miraculously, has enough time to leap for the side, but her lover goes under. There's a bit of thrashing around and a lot of bubbles, but after a while the guy is still and only his huge bum breaks the surface, at right angles to the ice.

The skater approaches the woman, who is numb with shock, covers her with his coat and takes out his mobile phone. "Hello: police?" he says. "There's been an accident by the pond. I think you should cordon off the area. The ice isn't safe; there's a huge crack in it."

Cue for joke

A bloke is visiting his folks in New York and one night decides to go and check out the local pool hall. His dad gives him an address and off he goes.

After a couple of hours, the son comes back, looking decidedly unhappy. He fetches himself a beer from the fridge and sprawls in the sofa.

"What's the matter?" the dad asks. "You didn't find the place?"

"Oh, I found the place all right," he replies. "It's great; typically American, with high ceilings and guys with gold teeth smoking cigars. Fantastic: all I ever wanted."

"So what's wrong?"

"Well, I'd been playing for a while when a guy came up to me and said he could beat me in two gotchas."

"What the hell is a gotcha?" the dad enquires.

"Well, that's what I asked. Anyway, he wouldn't tell me. I just carried on playing. I was pretty good. Then, just when I got a nice easy line-up, this guy just crept behind me and screamed 'Gotcha!' right in my ear. I was so surprised I thought I'd had a heart attack."

"That's a nasty trick to pull," dad remarked. "Still, that's only one gotcha. He did it again, I take it?"

"He didn't need to," the son replied. "I was crap after that. Do you have any idea how nervous you can get waiting for the next gotcha?"

For the birds

A pair of morons have signed up for a Holidays for Morons package and find themselves at the edge of a cliff, arms outstretched. One of them has ten budgies tightly wrapped around his arms, while the other has a few parrots glued to his back. They look at one another, vaguely wondering where the instructors have gone, close their eyes and jump. Sure enough, they land with a splat on the sandy beach below and are carted off to Accident and Emergency.
A couple of days later they wake up in adjoining hospital beds with all kinds of ropes and pulleys attached to their limbs.

"Well, I don't know about you," says one, "but I don't think much of budgie-jumping."

"Yeah: and that parrot-gliding's not all it's cracked up to be either."

Bill, please

A guy has booked a relaxing and healthy holiday in an activity resort in a bid to get rid of some flab the easy way. He checks in, dumps his bags on the bed and goes down to reception.

"Is it possible to play tennis here?" he asks.

"Sure," the receptionist replies. "We have ten courts at your disposal, and I'm sure I can find one that's free for you right now."

"That'd be great," the guy says. "I don't have any gear, though. How much will it cost me?"

"Nothing, sir," the girl replies. "Everything's included in the room. Just go to the store and sort yourself out some kit. I'll book you a court and find you a partner."

By the time the guy's got himself some trainers, a racquet and a pair of shorts, the receptionist has lined him up a court for the day and found him someone to play against. After a whole day spent playing tennis, the following day he decides to try scuba diving. Once again he learns everything's included, so he gets himself some gear and heads for the pond, where an instructor spends the day showing him the basics. The holiday drifts by in this way, trying riding, squash, archery, whitewater rafting and a whole lot of other activities, at no extra cost.

On the last day, the guy realises that he's tried just about everything on offer except golf, so he gives it a quick go. At the end of the morning he goes to the reception again to hand in his golf gear.

"How did it go, sir?"

"Not really well, I'm afraid," the guy replies. "It seems I'm not very good at golf. I lost five balls."

"Oh, I see," the receptionist says. She checks on a chart and says: "I'm afraid that'll be £5,000."

"What? I've been doing all these activities for free and now you're charging me £5,000?" the guy blubbers.

"Well, you know these hotels have you by the balls, sir."

A matter of life and death

Two old geezers are fishing in the local lake when a tourist zooms past on waterskis, drenching them and sending the rods fly. Shouts of "Arsehole" and "Peabrain" can be heard for a full five minutes, and then the old guys pick up their gear and cast their lines again, grumbling. Ten minutes later the young waterskier's back, this time in the opposite direction, sending more waves to splash the two codgers all over. The fishermen shake their fists, shout insults and so forth but the guy's already long gone, so they dry themselves, sit down and resume fishing as best they can. On the third pass, the young bloke loses his footing, slides off and drowns. One of the old guys sighs, takes off his boots and dives for him. A few seconds later he surfaces holding a body. "He's not breathing. I brought him up; it's your turn to give him mouth-to-mouth." The other bloke isn't very pleased, but old people have values and he starts trying to resuscitate the guy. Then...

"Eurgh!" the old man screams, spitting frantically. "He stinks!"

"What do you mean, he stinks?"

"Man, that's the worst breath I've ever smelled."

"Oh, come on; I'll do it," the other man says. He bends down, puts his mouth to the corpse's and instantly recoils.

"Oh, my God, he stinks!"

"Told you so," his friend says. Then a thought strikes him. "I wonder if you brought back the right one, you know, This one's wearing ice skates."

So that's all right, then

A parachute instructor tells his group of tourists: "I have to tell you that the fatal accident ratio in parachuting is one out of a thousand. But that doesn't apply to you, as there are only 15 of you."

One man and his dog

A businessman is sitting next to a blind man on a plane. The businessman doesn't really like flying. He's very nervous: so nervous, in fact, that the blind man somehow senses it.

"You don't like flying, do you?" he says to the businessman with an encouraging smile.

"I hate it," the guy replies between clenched teeth, "but you seem to be taking to it all right."

"Oh, I love flying," the blind man says. "In fact, my favourite sport's skydiving."

"Skydiving? How? I mean, I don't want to appear rude, but a man in your condition: how do you do it?"

"There's no special requirement," the blind man explains, "though of course in my case, it requires a bit of planning and a special dog."

"You skydive with a dog?"

"Oh yes. It's a special dog that's been trained to jump out of a plane. We jump together."

"I never imagined such a thing was possible," says the businessman in wonder. "But tell me; how do you know you're going to land?"

"Easy: when we're near the ground, the leash goes slack."

Left a bit

A woman is playing golf in Portugal. The weather is perfect but the sun, unfortunately, is in her eyes, so much so that she swings and misses her shot totally. The ball, instead of gracefully arcing its way to the green, violently hits the player in front of her. Horrified, she sees him slowly collapsing to the ground, his hands between his legs.

She rushes over to the guy and finds him rocking gently in a foetal position on the grass.

"I'm a physiotherapist; I can help," she says to the bloke. "Please let me do something."

The bloke is in no position to say no and soon she's got her hand in his trousers, expertly stroking his balls.

"How does that feel?" she asks after a few minutes.

"Yeah, that's great. My thumb still hurts, though."

It happened so quickly

This guy has won a skydiving weekend: one of those adventure day packages. He's quite thrilled but a bit afraid, and is masking his fear by asking silly questions and being cocky.

"So, tell me," he asks the instructor, "if the primary 'chute doesn't open and the reserve one doesn't open either, how long do we have until we hit the ground?"

The instructor looks him square in the eye and replies, deadpan: "The rest of your life, sir."

Too true

Two women friends are relaxing in a bar after a morning's skiing.

"You know, I've always thought men were a bit like snow," says the first one.

"How so?" her friend replies.

"Well, you never know how many inches you're going to get or how long it's going to last."

Occupational hazard

Did you hear about the moron who went elephant-hunting on holiday? He got a hernia carrying the decoys.

Get in shape

You know you've made the right decision to take up jogging on holiday if, on your first try at it, you have more jiggle than jog.

The ultimate betrayal

A businessman is having a steamy affair with his secretary. Quite often their passion compels them to leave the office, drive to her house and screw like rabbits. Today that's exactly what they've done, but the sex is so good and lasts so long they fall asleep. When he wakes up, the businessman realises with horror that it's already eight in the evening. He imagines his wife waiting for him all evening and his dinner getting cold in the oven. Putting his clothes on, he asks his mistress to quickly smear his shoes with soil and dirt from her garden. The woman's nonplussed but she does as she's told and, with a last kiss, the businessman rushes back home.

"Where have you been?" his wife asks him, her voice on that side of frosty.

"You know I can't lie to you, honey," the man says contritely. "I had an afternoon of rampant sex with my secretary and we've only just woken up."

The wife, her eyes like slits, points at his shoes and says: "You lying bastard! You've been playing golf with your mates again!"

Wise words

Tourist with unchecked parachute will leap to conclusion.

They're just like us

If you go on holiday in Africa, you will discover that some tribes have a custom of beating the ground with clubs and uttering spine-chilling cries. Anthropologists call this a form of primitive performance art. In Britain we call it golf.

Man's best friend

An American bloke is sitting at the counter in a Spanish bar with his dog.

"I'll bet you a round of drinks my dog can talk," he says.

"Yeah? Sure; go ahead," the bartender says.

The guy turns to his dog and asks: "What covers a house?" The dog says: "Roof!"

"How does sandpaper feel?"

"Rough!"

"Who was the greatest baseball player of all time?" The dog says: "Ruth!"

With a grin, the guy turns to the barman and says: "Come on; pay up. I told you he could talk."

The barman grunts and throws them both out of the door. Sitting on the pavement while his owner is brushing himself down, the dog looks across at him and says: "Should I have said Gehrig, then?"

Easily confused

A dyslexic couple go on a skiing holiday. They're having a great time, but sometimes argue about whether they're zigzagging or zagzigging. One evening, as they're having yet another barney in the ski shop, the husband decides to ask the assistant to settle their dispute.

"You're a true native, so you must know," he says. "When skiing, do you zigzag or do you zagzig?"

"How should I know?" the guy replies. "I hate skiing. I'm a tobogganist. "

"Oh," the man says. "Never mind. Thanks anyway. Actually, while I'm here, give us 20 Silk Cut."

Now that's impressive

A martial artist is off to Japan for a samurai competition. He's pretty good, but he doesn't fool himself: there is no way he can successfully compete with the local guys. Sure enough, he doesn't even pass the first day of tournament. It doesn't really matter though, as he has a great time watching the Japanese martial artists show their skills. Soon there are only three guys left to compete: a Chinese samurai, a Japanese samurai and a Jewish samurai.

The Chinese samurai steps forward, takes out his sword and, with a mighty swish, cuts a passing fly in two. The crowd is ecstatic and roars its appreciation.

The second contestant steps forward and, with a swish that's like the wind howling through the steppes, he cuts a passing fly in four perfectly equal parts. The crowd is now crazy; everybody is jumping and chanting the name of the Japanese samurai.

The Jewish contestant steps forward and takes his sword out. There follows a series of swishes and acrobatic movements but the insect simply flies past him.

The Chinese and Japanese samurai sneer. "You didn't manage to kill the little fly," they scoff. "Circumcision isn't meant to kill," the Jewish samurai says, unruffled.

Thanks anyway

An extremely old geezer has been offered membership of a golf club by his son. Unfortunately, even though the old guy can still swing a club, his eyesight's not what it used to be and he can't really see where the ball goes.

"It's hopeless," he says to his wife. "I'd say I was still a decent golfer, but I just can't follow the ball any more."

"Why don't you take your brother with you?"

"Mark? But he doesn't even play golf!" the old timer scoffs.

"Well, maybe not, but he's got excellent eyesight. He'll tell you where the ball goes."

The man thinks about it and has to admit that his wife might actually have had a good idea. A few days later, he goes back to the club and starts a game.

"All you need to do is keep your eyes on the ball. Don't look anywhere else," he says to his brother. Mark agrees and the old guy swings the perfect shot.

"Can you se it? Can you see it? Don't lose it!"

"Yeah, I can see it; no worries."

"Ok; where is it now?"

Mark turns around to his brother, starts to speaks, turns around again and squints into the distance, then says: "I forgot."

Damn!

A guy is confronting his wife with a plan he's not sure she's going to agree to.

"Honey, I've been invited for a week's fishing in Scotland by the company. It's part of a new scheme to promote teamwork, staff development and stuff, you know?"

"Mmm," his wife says noncommittally.

"Erm," the bloke continues, ill at ease. "I'd really like to go. All my colleagues will be there, and my line manager and my boss. It'd look pretty bad If I couldn't make it, you know?"

"I see," his wife says with a smile. "Of course you can go. I don't want to interfere with your career."

The guy breathes a sigh of relief and soon he's off to Scotland. As his wife suspected, there's very little fishing involved during his week there. Instead he's in the pub morning, afternoon and evening, telling raucous stories, playing snooker and smoking.

When he's back, his wife asks how the trip went.

"Oh, great!" the man says with a grin. "You forgot to pack my pyjamas, though."

"I didn't forget, honey," the wife replies sweetly. "I put them in your tackle box."

The obvious answer

A guy is on a scuba dive in the Red Sea. The sea floor is marvellous, covered in multicoloured plants and corals, and the waters are teaming with shiny, exotic fish. He's been diving for fifteen minutes when he passes a man who's not wearing a mask or a tank. The diver's surprised; he didn't know you could dive so deep without any gear. He nods to the other bloke and heads a bit deeper. To his astonishment, he immediately meets the same guy again, still not wearing any gear. Puzzled, he picks up his slate and writes: "I didn't know you could dive so deep without a mask on."

The other man reads the slate, takes it from him and writes: "I'm drowning, you arsehole."

Dog day afternoon

It's the summer holidays and the weather in London is stifling. This doesn't prevent a couple of lads from having a scratch game of football in Finsbury Park. All of a sudden a pit bull terrier, driven crazy by the heat and the shouts of sheer delight coming from the youngsters, escapes his master's grip and rushes over to launch a savage attack on one of the players.

The other lad, after a stunned pause, looks around and quickly grabs a big stone, which he drops with all his might on the head of the dog. The dog dies instantly.

Fortunately, a reporter is on the scene and sees everything: a boy screaming, a lad trying to ease his pain and the dog's owner crying over the body of his canine chum. The reporter takes his pad out of his pocket and walks over to the lad.

"Congratulations; that was some quick thinking there," he says to him, jotting down, "Arsenal fan rescues friend from rabid dog" on his pad.

"I'm not an Arsenal fan," the boy says, glancing at the pad.

"Sorry?"

"I'm not an Arsenal fan."

"Oh, come on; you're playing in Finsbury Park, you're bright and young, you've got to be an Arsenal fan!"

"Well, as a matter of fact I support Man U," the boy says defiantly. The reporter stares at him for a couple of seconds and tears off the page from his pad. On a fresh page, he writes: "Man U fan murders beloved family pet."

I'm not being funny but ...

Three friends, a priest, a doctor and an engineer, meet for a weekend of golf. They rent a room near the club and are now waiting for a hole to come free; the players ahead of them are taking ages. After half an hour, just when the three men are starting to loose patience, a bloke from the group in front walks over to them.

"I'm sorry," he says. "I'm accompanying a group of blind firefighters. They were called out to a job two weeks ago and the whole building blew up. They're heroes here, and the club decided to grant them free use of the facilities as part of a new psychological treatment to help them cope with their disability."

"How sad, and so great a sacrifice," the priest says piously. "We should pray for their soul and for the souls of all the good men in the world."

"I have a friend who's a very famous ophthalmologist. I'm sure he could help," the doctor says.

The engineer grumbles, "Well, yeah, it's all very nice, but why can't they play at night?"

A ray of hope

Saddam Hussein's lawyer goes to visit him in his cell and tells him: "Saddam, I have some good news and some bad news."

"OK; tell me the bad news first."

"Well, you've been convicted of crimes against humanity and you're going to be put in front of a firing squad."

"Wow," Saddam whistles. "And what possible good news can there be?"

"It's Beckham who going to shoot."

CHAPTER EIGHT

Travel Jokes

A Hemingway moment

A little boy rushes into a general store in Spain. In broken Spanish, he tries to explain that his dad is being chased by an enraged bull.

"El toro? I am calling the police – emergency!" the manager exclaims.

"No, it's OK," the little boy says. "I just wanted some film for my camera."

You can help by not helping

A blonde is on holiday in northern Italy, in the Alps. She's minding her own business, driving her car to the resort, when she has to stop at a red light. She then notices that the lorry in front of her is losing its cargo on the road. Wanting to do a good deed, she steps out of the car and knocks on the truck window.

"Hi, I'm Stacey and you're losing your load on the road!"

The truck driver looks at her blankly. The light turns to green and he moves on. Undeterred, and putting everything down to her bad Italian accent, the blonde gets back in her car too. At the next red light, she climbs out, bangs on the truck window again and shouts: "Hi, I'm Stacey and you're losing your load on the road! Can you understand?"

The driver shakes his head and drives off. Furious, the blonde gets back into her car, slams the door and follows the truck to the next red light.

Out she gets again, and this time she stands in front of the truck yelling: "Hi, I'm Stacey and you're losing your load on the road!"

"Hi, I'm Guiseppe," the driver replies in an exasperated tone, "and I'm driving a gritting lorry!"

Law of the jungle

Two friends have gone on a holiday tour of the jungles of South America. They are really enjoying the mosquitoes, the weird food and the local culture. They eat insects; they learn rude words in Portuguese and do white-water rafting. They're having a wonderful time, when one day a deep, unmistakable growl informs them that there is a jaguar somewhere near. They stare at one another in panic; then one of them suddenly throws his backpack on the ground, searches through it frantically and pulls out a pair of trainers.

"You don't really think you're going to be faster than the jaguar wearing those, do you?" the first guy asks incredulously.

"Oh, no," his friend replies, taking to his heels, "but I don't need to be faster than the jaguar; I just need to be faster than you!"

God sees all

A pious couple are touring Scotland. They visit the local churches with their quaint decorations and imposing settings and soon notice that they're all circular. What at first they thought was a strange local custom seems to be widespread and they can't understand it. After a week, they decide to ask a local vicar about it.

"Excuse me, Father," the spouse says reverently, "we've noticed that all the churches here are round. I mean, I don't want to criticise the architecture and I find them lovely, but, er... why?"

The vicar looks around suspiciously, squints at the couple and, satisfied that they are indeed tourists, replies: "Remember, you're in Scotland. The church is round so that my flock doesn't have anywhere to hide when it's time for the donation."

Never too old

A young couple are sitting in front of a much older couple on the train. The young ones are all over one another and don't stop kissing. The older woman turns to her husband and, with a knowing smile, says: "See? This is what you should be doing."

The old codger looks her up and down and replies: "I don't know that young woman!"

Facts of life

Two young women are sitting by the poolside, checking the guys over. One leans over to the other and says: "You know the perfect sizes for a man?"

"No; tell me," the other replies, giggling.

"80, 20, 42."

"What do you mean?" the girl asks, puzzled.

"80 years old, £20 million in the bank and a 42-degree fever."

Love, honour and... oh, boy

This couple decide to get married abroad. Everything goes as scheduled, except at the end, when it's time to give some money to the church. The groom approaches the priest and whisper in his ear: "Er, Father, how does it work here: I mean, for the donation? How much are we supposed to give?"

The priest, not really wanting to ask for money straight out, finds an elegant way to put it: "It entirely depends on how pretty the bride is."

The groom, delighted, sees an opportunity to save some cash. He fishes a one-euro coin from his pocket and hands it to the priest with a big smile. The priest, without missing a beat, looks at the coin and says: "Thank you, my son. I'll bring you the change shortly."

The lonely sea and the sky

"Ah, now I know I'm in Scotland!" a husband exclaims to his wife, while they're taking a stroll along the beach at Nairn.

"Why do you say that, honey? We've been in Scotland for a week!"

The husband points to a fishing boat out at sea. "You see that? There isn't one seagull following it. That's how I know I'm really in Scotland."

Chow time

A man enters a Texas bar leading a crocodile on a leash.

"Howdy! Say, you serve English people here?"

"Yeah, we serve everyone; this is a free country," the barman replies.
"OK, then. Give me a beer and an Englishman."

Let's think about this

A man is waiting for his wife in a hotel lounge. She turns up, all dressed up, and orders a martini.
"I've had my credit card stolen," says the husband.
"Oh, my God! This is terrible! Did you report it to the police?"
"Don't be silly. The thief'll probably spend less than you do."

Unscheduled stopover

On a plane, a man is sitting at a window seat next to a blonde. After an hour or so, he needs to go to the toilet so he gets up and queues for a while, waiting for the cubicle to come free. When he comes back, he's annoyed to see that the blonde's now sitting in his seat. He approaches and clears his throat.
"Excuse me, but you've pinched my seat," he says with an engaging but firm smile.
The blonde looks around, blushes to the roots of her hair and mumbles: "Oh, I'm so sorry; I thought you'd got off."

And what's your point?

They say that men only think about sex, but that's not really true. They also think about football, beer and going on holiday once a year.

The mysterious Orient

A European finds himself in a Chinese prison. Bewildered, the victim of a super-quick trial during which he hasn't understood a single word, he is sitting in his cell, stunned, when he hears scratching to his right. He keeps still and, after a while, realises that there is someone on the other side of the wall. Seizing his shoe, he taps back and the other prisoner asks him a question in rapid-fire Chinese.

"I'm sorry; I don't understand. I don't speak Chinese," the bloke says, in tears.

"Oh, speak English, hey?"

"Yes, yes; I speak English!"

"How long you have in here?"

"I think ten years; that's what I think I understood."

"Ten years?" the other prisoner exclaims. "What you have done?"

"Nothing!"

"You must done something. Nothing, here only five year."

Our furry friends

A guy walks into a bar down in Alabama and orders a Pimm's. Surprised, the bartender leans over the counter and looks at him.

"You're not from around here, are you?" he sneers.

"That's correct; I'm British. I live in London" the guy replies.

The bartender frowns. "What do you do there?"

"I'm a taxidermist," comes the reply.

"A taxidermist?" he cries. "What the hell is a taxidermist?"

"I mount dead animals."

The bartender smiles and turns to the rest of the bar. "It's OK, boys," he shouts. "He's one of us!"

Hammer and tongs

An Italian, an American and a Frenchman are talking about sex. More particularly, they are talking about how much their respective wives love the way they make love to them.

The Italian says: "Last night I made love to my wife three times. She came three times and told me I was the best lover she'd ever had."

The American says: "Last night I made love to my wife four times. When we were done, she said she wouldn't be able to love anyone more than she loved me and then she fell asleep, exhausted."

"Last night I made love to my wife once," the Frenchman says.

"Once only?" the Italian and American sneer. "And what did she have to say about it in the morning?"

"'Don't stop.'"

Near miss

On the Costa Brava, a very attractive young lady walks up to the bar and calls over the barman, a tall fellow with a thick, full beard. The woman leans over the bar in her low-cut dress and reaches out to touch the man.

"Are you the landlord?" she asks, gently stroking his lustrous beard and running her fingers through his hair.

"No," gulps the barman, "I just work here."

"Well," says the forward young lady, caressing the barman's beard with both hands. "Can I talk to him?"

"Er, no," says the by now highly excited barman. "He's not here tonight."

"Well, when you see him," the blonde purrs, gently caressing the barman's face, "tell him there's no toilet roll in the ladies'."

Wrong question

A couple have gone to Brazil for a holiday, but are having trouble with the heat. They're in a bus taking them to a remote village and are sweating profusely. They ride through superb landscape and wild vegetation, but all they can think about is a cold shower – something they're quite certain isn't waiting for them at their destination.

To their delight, however, on arriving they spot a river not far from the village. They quickly dump their stuff in their hut, put on their jungle-stripe bathing suits and, half-delirious with expectation, run to the river.

Just before plunging into the water, though, the husband has a doubt. He looks around and sees a group of kids idly sitting by a rickety bridge.

"Hiya, kids," he greets them. "Any crocodiles around here?"

"No, Mister; no crocodile."

"You're sure? I was told there were crocodiles everywhere in Brazil."

"No crocodiles here, Mister!"

Reassured, the husband turns to his wife with a big grin and they both dash forwards, failing to hear the kid saying to one of his mates: "I haven't seen a crocodile in here since the piranhas ate them all."

Culture clash

A British vicar is sent to New York by his congregation. Before he leaves, he has a debriefing with the Bishop.

"Dear Vicar, it's a joy for us to send you to the US of A and see how they deal with religion over there," he says. "Hopefully, you might be able to put into practice here some of what you will learn over there and find a way to bring up the numbers at our little church."

The Bishop takes a sip of his brandy and carries on, "You have to be careful, though. Be wary of the press. I contacted the church authorities in America and they know you're coming, and it will be seen as a minor media event, what with the rocky times we're all going through at present."

The vicar promises to be careful and not to draw too much attention to himself.

On his arrival in Newark, he's surprised to see a news reporter waiting for him with a microphone.

"So, Vicar, are you going to visit any of the nightclubs in New York?" the reporter asks mischievously.

"Are there any nightclubs in New York?" the vicar replies, feigning innocence and trying to defuse any further awkward questions. The reporter shrugs and packs his bags, leaving the vicar with the impression that he's handled the situation pretty well.

The vicar takes a taxi to his hotel and waits sedately for the church officials to pick him up for a tour of the local religious amenities. He waits and waits and finally phones the reception.

"Oh, yes, sir; we've just received a package for you," the receptionist says. "Could you please come down and collect it?"

Puzzled, the vicar takes the lift down to reception, where he is handed a large brown envelope. Opening it, he is flabbergasted to realise that it contains a return ticket for a flight leaving in a couple of hours. There is nothing else in the envelope but a newspaper cutting, which reads: "Still standing on the tarmac at Newark, vicar asks if there are any nightclubs in New York!"

Seeking clarification

The invisible man to the invisible girl: "Do you still live with your transparents?"

Sticky situation

A scientist is on holiday in Brazil. He's happily cataloguing the wildlife and picking samples of vegetation on his leisure walks when one day he stumbles across a pond. A pond is a magnet for scientists and soon the old fool, instead of investigating the local population and the customs, decides instead to study the mating habits of the resident frogs. He quickly comes to the conclusion that the population is dwindling. It seems there's something in the water, maybe some household waste which makes the frogs' skin oily so they can't cling together and copulate effectively. Puzzled, the scientist spends the reminder of his holidays trying different mixtures in order to change the viscosity of the water. It is only near the end of his vacation that he finds the correct combination: some algal extract, chemicals of some sort and a pinch of salt.

"Who would have thought it?" he thinks to himself happily, watching the frogs copulate like crazy. "They need monosodium glue to mate."

Dirty business

In the jungle, two tigers are walking along in single file. Suddenly, the tiger behind licks the arse of the tiger in front.
"Oi – stop that!"

"Sorry," the tiger says and they carry on their silent journey through the jungle. Ten minutes pass and the tiger behind once again licks the arse of the tiger in front.
"I said stop that!" the first tiger shouts. "What's the matter with you, anyway?"

"I've just eaten a lawyer and I'm trying to get the taste out of my mouth," the second tiger says.

No time like the present

The captain of the plane has to do something he's never done in his life: order the crew to prepare the passengers for an emergency landing. As the plane descends in a series of sickening, shuddering plunges, the senior flight attendant reports back to the cockpit.

"Is everybody ready?" the captain grunts, trying to keep control of the plane.

"Yes; everyone has assumed the crash-landing position except for a lawyer who's still passing around business cards," she replies.

Man's best friend

Three hunters – a doctor, an engineer and a lawyer – are on holiday, staying in a boarding house. They're paired up for a day's hunting and take an instant dislike to one another, but decide to make the best of it and set off into the forest together, only to stumble on a clearing full of bones. Seizing this opportunity to show off, the doctor turns to his fellow-hunters and says: "See that pile of bones there? I'll show you what a real hunting dog can do." He then bends down to his dog and say: "Bones. Go get the bones."

The dog barks once, dashes forward, picks up some bones and in no time has built a human skeleton out of them. His master is delighted.

"Not bad," the engineer says. "Now have a look at this." He kneels down to speak to his dog: "Bones. Go get them."

The dog yaps once, runs forward and promptly builds a replica of the Eiffel Tower, complete with a moving lift. The engineer stands up, beaming at the others, but the lawyer is clearly not impressed. With a sneer, he turns to his dog and says: "Bones."

The dog looks up, nods, tears down the replica of the Eiffel Tower, eats half the bones, buries the other half, thoroughly screws the other two dogs and takes the rest of the afternoon off.

On a wing and a prayer

This is the fourth time the prototype of a brand-new plane has been tested. The past three tests have yielded terrible results, as the plane has never been able to take off, its right wing tearing off at exactly the same place each time. The engineers are understandably edgy and more than one is thinking that their very job is on the line now: this damned plane has to take off this time.

The control tower gives its go-ahead, the engines are rumbling, the plane looks sleek and efficient, the lines audacious... here it goes, speeding down the runway – and, with a deafening noise, the right wing is ripped away from the rest of the body and flutters away in tatters.

The engineers don't understand. All their calculations seem correct and they can't figure out what's going wrong.

One of the team, dejected, drags himself to the toilet. He needs some time on his own. He takes a good look in the mirror, as if trying to inspect the interior of his brain to find a solution. At this moment, the janitor appears.

"So that's the fourth time, is it?"

"Yeah," the engineer sighs.

"Would you be offended if I gave you a piece of advice?"

The engineer laughs hysterically. "No, go ahead; anything will make more sense than what's happening right now."

"Well, I was thinking, maybe you should drill a line of holes where the wing rips off," the janitor says.

"What?"

"Just a series of little holes. I'm sure it'd help; trust me."

"Tiny holes. In the body of the plane. Where the wing breaks. Right. You're out of your mind."

The engineer storms out and heads off home, a great weight on his mind. He gets into bed, still trying to solve the problem of the breaking wing, and the words of the janitor keep intruding. Holes in the plane: silly... but then again, what has he got to lose? They've tried everything. This janitor's been around for ever; maybe another team of engineers came across the same problem a long time ago and that was how they got round it. In the morning, the engineer has made his decision: he's got a week to put a wing back on the prototype and drill some little holes along it where it joins the rest of the plane.

A week later, the prototype is back on the runway. The janitor and the engineer are sitting next to one another when the take-off clearance is given and the plane starts its run. It's a success. The plane takes off with no problem, all the wings stay dutifully attached to it, it cruises at a fantastic speed; in short, the plane is doing everything it was designed to do.

The engineer, dizzy with relief, clasps the janitor's hands and demands: "Now, tell me; why these little holes?"

"Well, you see," the janitor explains, "I've been working them toilets for years and I can tell you one thing: I've never seen the toilet paper tear along the dotted lines."

Technical hitch

Two blondes are on a flight from London to New York. Fifteen minutes into the trip, the captain announces: "I'm sorry, but as you can see if you look out of the port side windows, we've lost an engine. However, we're flying a very good plane. Three engines will do fine and we're not in immediate danger, but the flight will take a little bit longer."

Fifteen minutes later, the captain announces the loss of another engine. "We can make it with only two engines, but I'm sorry that the trip's going to be a rather longer one. We can expect around two hours' delay."

Fifteen minutes later, the captain announces the loss of yet another engine and the increase of the delay to four hours. One blonde looks at the other and complains: "If we lose one more engine, we'll be up here all day."

Have him disinfected and brought to my tent

A rich film star is working in Australia. She's hot and sweaty and the Outback isn't as romantic as she thought it would be. The shoot's boring and after a few days she asks her assistant to find her some local entertainment. "I want a virgin this time," she says. "I'm fed-up screwing men who always think they know better. Bring me someone who's never been with a woman before."

The assistant is nonplussed, but does her best. It takes her a couple of days, but she does manage to find a virgin male who's not too bad-looking, even by Australian standards, and leads him to the door of the film star's trailer.

The guy enters the trailer and immediately moves the sofa against the door, stacks the coffee table to one side and removes the fluffy carpet.

"What on earth are you doing?" the diva asks.

"Well, it's true I've never shagged a woman," he says, "but if it's anything like shagging a kangaroo, we'll need plenty of room."

Straight talking

An old woman is sitting in a train travelling from France to Switzerland. Seeing that the train is slowing down before the customs, she says to the priest sharing her carriage: "Could you do me a favour and hide this little vanity case I bought under your clothes? I mean, it's only beauty creams and things, but if I could avoid paying taxes on it..."

"I'll hide this for you, my child, but remember that I cannot lie."

"It's all right, Father; you won't have to."

The train stops in the station and a policeman from the customs office enters the carriage. He asks the priest if he has anything to declare.

"No, officer: nothing to declare above the waist."

"Oh: and do you have anything to declare below the waist?" the officer asks, his curiosity piqued by the priest's statement.

"Oh, only a little something for ladies that hasn't been used yet."

French letters

A dad and his son are in Nice.

"Oh, look at those boats!" the boy exclaims.

"They're nice, aren't they? They're called yachts."

"Yachts? How do you spell that?"

"Mmmm... you're right after all. They're boats."

Kill or cure

A motorcyclist and his pillion passenger are touring the Alps on a great big bike. The weather's pretty poor and the wind's howling. The guy at the back has decided to wear his jacket back to front, to be better protected from the wind.

After half an hour's riding , the driver shouts to his passenger: "You OK?" There's no answer. He shouts again, to no avail. Glancing back quickly, he realises his friend isn't on the bike any more. Panicking, he does a U-turn and speeds back down the road to find him. Sure enough, after a few kilometres he stumbles upon a crowd of people surrounding a pair of cars with flashing lights. He stops the bike and puts it on its stand, and is about to introduce himself to the police and confess that he's lost his pillion when he hears one of the policemen say: "OK, now; on the count of three, we turn his head back the right way. One, two..."

Home truths

The boss has had a good and profitable lunch and comes back to work in a rare good humour. He's in such a good mood, in fact, that he's even telling a few jokes to his staff. Everyone is laughing with him except a bored-looking secretary.

"Why aren't you laughing?" he asks her.

"I don't have to," she replies. "I'm off to Ibiza at five."

Nearer, my God, to thee

The Pope has just finished a visit to France and is escorted back to Charles de Gaulle airport by car. He's feeling a bit mischievous and decides to have a go at driving the limousine which has been assigned to him. He asks his driver to climb in the back and off they go. They join the motorway and the Pope decides to check out the limo, and starts accelerating a little bit. Soon he's lost his escort and is speeding down the motorway, having the time of his life.

No one can escape the French motorway police, though. A young cop catches up with him and flashes his lights, indicating that the Pope had better pull over on the emergency lane, which the Pope does.

The young policeman walks up to the driver's window and the colour drains from his face; he instantly recognises the Pope. Unsure how to handle the situation, he walks back to his car and radios his superior.

"Er... Commander, I have a little problem. I've just stopped this car for speeding but I'm afraid it's somebody pretty important."

"Who is it? A councillor?"

"Er... higher, sir."

"A minister, then?"

"Still higher, sir."

"Higher than a minister? It can't be the President, can it?"

"Er, no, sir. Someone higher."

"Higher than the President? You're pulling my leg, aren't you?"

"No, sir! I don't know who this guy is, but his chauffeur's the Pope!"

Halting unexpectedly

A guy with a stammer is travelling by train but has fallen asleep and, waking, isn't sure whether he's missed his stop. The train is stopped at a station, he can't see a sign and so turns to one of his neighbours and asks: "So...so... sorry, is... is this Do... Do... Dover?" The bloke doesn't reply. The guy asks again: "So...so... sorry, is... is this Do... Do... Dover?" Still the guy doesn't reply. The other passenger is about to answer when a voice is heard through the PA: "Dover Priory, Dover Priory!" The guy with the speech impediment scowls at the other guy, gathers his suitcases and dashes out.

"Why didn't you reply to him? That wasn't very nice of you," the other passenger admonishes.

"I... I didn't... have ti...ti... time... and I'm mmmmmm... sure he would...would...have... b...b...b... beaten me up," he replies.

Mean streets

This guy gets a puncture right in the middle of a dodgy area of Hackney. He stops on the kerb, switches the engine off and starts cranking up the back of the car. A white van passes the car, then slams on the brakes, reverses and parks right in front of the car. A shaved-head punk in a bomber jacket picks up a baseball bat from the back of the van, walks to the car and smashes the windscreen.

"You get the tyres and I get the stereo," he says.

Keep one handy

A guy has rented a Harley for a couple of weeks to tour Italy. He stops at a roadside café for a can of Coke and starts polishing his bike while sipping his drink. He's using Vaseline, as it's waterproof and is good to keep the chrome shiny. His cleaning over, he revs the engine a couple of times, just to annoy the local Vespas, and off he goes.

On the way, he picks up a charming hitchhiker. They can't really chat over the noise of the engine, but they manage to communicate enough for the bloke to understand that he's being invited to the girl's house to have lunch with her and her parents.

The bloke parks the bike in front of the house. "One thing: you mustn't speak while we're having lunch. If you speak, you'll have to do the washing-up and I have plans for you afterwards and I don't want to be late," she says suggestively.

The motorcyclist finds this a bit strange, but agrees. He's welcomed like a prince; the mother piles up spaghetti on his plate and the father pours him Chianti, all done without a word.

The girl keeps on playing footsie with him and glancing at him seductively. After a glass of wine, the guy can't take it any more. He stands up, walks around to where the girl is sitting and leans over her. He kisses her passionately while his hand plunges down into her blouse. The father gulps, but says nothing. Grinning inwardly, the bloke picks up the girl, turns her around, lifts her skirt up and screws her shamelessly over the table, all this without uttering a sound. The parents are apoplectic but they too remain silent. The other daughters are trying their best not to giggle, placing their hands in front of their mouths and staring at the action taking place in front of their very eyes.

The motorcyclist finishes with the girl, drains his glass of Chianti, leers at the first sister and, quick as a flash, starts screwing her too. The second sister succumbs to the silent sex in her turn a few minutes later. Sated, the biker burps, gets dress in silence and picks up the tub of Vaseline from his pocket.

"I'll do the washing-up; I'll do the washing-up!" squeals the father.

What do you mean, you haven't read it?

The Lord has decided that what the world really needs is another downpour. It worked before and he doesn't see any point in changing the tried and tested formula, so he goes and finds the descendant of Noah on earth.

"I need you to build an ark," the Lord says to him. "You know the drill."

Noah's descendant nods. He spends ten years building his ark and it's ready when the rain comes. It rains for forty days and forty nights. When it's over, the Lord is pleased and instructs Noah's great-great-great grandson to release the animals.

"The what?" he asks.

"The animals you have in your ark," replies God.

"I don't have any animals; I'm a vegetarian."

"What have you got in there, then?" the Good Lord asks, appalled.

"Two tomatoes, two broccoli, two potatoes..."

Highly trained

A family is waiting to go through the customs at Folkestone.

"Did you know that there are two ways you could become a customs officer?" the husband asks his wife. "You either go to university or you go to vocational college."

"Oh, really? And how do you see the difference?" the wife wonders.

"If they went to college, they let you through with a wave. If they went to university, they let you through with a nod," he replies.

Reach the beach

This guy is nearing the end of his holiday. Every day, he's taken a walk along the beach and today, as usual, some way out to sea there's a little kid with no arms who's fighting his way towards the shore.

The guy waits for the boy to make it to land and congratulates him.

"You're a very good swimmer."

"Thanks, sir. I have a lot of practice."

"Yes, I noticed that; you come here every day, don't you?"

"Yes; my dad's got a little dinghy and he drops me off every morning."

"You're very brave. It must be very hard for you because of your disability."

"Oh, that's nothing, sir. I have no problem swimming to shore. No; the hardest bit is getting out of the plastic bag."

Worth every penny

A very pretty young woman has been arrested for speeding in Greece. At her trial the lawyer, aware that Greek laws are very harsh on this type of offence, has to think out of the box.

"Members of the jury, please have a good look at this woman. Can you see how fragile she looks, how her skin glows, how full of life her tanned body is? Now, you have a choice. Either you put her away in a smelly, damp and cold jail, or you send her back to the Hotel Apollo, room 225, last door on the left on the second floor."

Terminal velocity

A plane is getting ready to take off. It joins the runway, gains some speed... and suddenly slows down, turns around and goes back to the gate it started from. A couple of hours pass and a passenger, his patience exhausted, hails a flight attendant.

"What's the hold-up? We've been waiting here for two hours. Why did we turn around?"

"Oh, it's nothing," the flight attendant replies. "The pilot was bothered by a noise he didn't like the sound of, and it takes a while to find a new pilot."

It could happen to anyone

A guy takes his rental car to the garage with a puncture.

"No problem; we'll have it repaired in no time," the mechanic says. He has a look at the tyre and, stroking his chin, continues: "Actually, it looks like you've got a cut here. Did you drive over some glass?"

"Yeah: over a bottle."

"And you didn't see it?"

"Nah; it was in some bum's pocket."

A long way down

A man taking a flight is surprised to see the seat next to him occupied by a parrot. They nod to one another, the bloke straps himself him and they take off.

When the plane is in the air, the parrot suddenly stops a passing flight attendant and shouts; "Bring me a whisky, you fat cow!"

The flight attendant is not amused, but the client is king and she brings the parrot a whisky. Some time later, the parrot stops the same flight attendant and shouts: "Hey, old tart, what does it take to get a drink in this joint?" The woman looks incensed, but still brings the parrot another whisky.

The bloke, who could do with a drink himself, considers what he's witnessed. Usually it takes ages to get served, but the parrot's methods have proved successful, so why not give it a try? He hails the same flight attendant: "Oi: you fucking bitch! Move your arse and get me a martini, will you?"

The woman looks at him with utter contempt and signals a beast of a security guy, who picks up both the man and the parrot and throws them out of the plane. As the bloke sees the ground rushing up to meet him, the parrot looks him over in open admiration. "For someone who can't fly, you've got balls!"

Chance of a lifetime

A husband has always wanted to go on a plane. Every time he broaches the subject to his wife though, he gets the same answer; it's too expensive. "A tenner's a tenner," she says, and then launches into a diatribe about how badly the window in the upstairs toilet needs new curtains.

One day there's an air show nearby and the husband manages to persuade his wife to go. "Look; it's free! Come on; at least I can watch."

The husband watches the planes take off and loop the loop and the desire to be there, to go and kiss the clouds, is getting stronger and stronger, to the point where he and his wife end up having an argument. A pilot, overhearing their heated conversation, walks up to them.

"Tell you want," he offers. "I'll fly you both – on one condition. You mustn't speak: not a word. If you don't speak, the ride's on me. If you do, you fork out £100."

The wife stubbornly refuses (a tenner's a tenner), but this time she's beaten down by the husband and off they go. The pilot has a field day: loops, dives, rolls, the lot. His passengers don't utter a peep, though, and he can see he's going to end up out of pocket.

Back on terra firma, the pilot shakes the man's hand. "So you did it!" he congratulates the guy. "You've been flying: and for free, too. You never said a word."

"Well, I nearly said something when the wife fell out, but a tenner's a tenner."

To chav and chav not

Two adjacent cottages in southern France have been bought by two different families. On the left is a bank director, his wife and his daughter and on the right is a chav family with three sons, a daughter and a stepdaughter. The two families meet for the first time.

"Nice place, innit?" the chav guy says. "I love these cottages, especially since mine's worth twice as much as yours."

"How so?" the bank manager enquires, surprised. "They're both the same!"

"Yeah, but I happen to live next to a bank manager, while you're stuck next to a load of chavs!"

Excuse me, sonny...

A plane is about to take off. It's the perfect moment for a little boy to throw a tantrum and little Billy does exactly that: he starts screaming, kicks the seat and flails his arms around – in brief, making an absolute pest of himself. His mum tries to calm him down, without much success. She's obviously struggling when an old man, in military uniform, walks up to her from the back of the plane. He silences the mother with a frown and shows Billy his medals and decorations, whispering something to him. The boy instantly stops screaming, calms down and obediently fastens his seatbelt.

An hour or so later, when the plane's cruising at 35,000 feet and little Billy's fast asleep, the mother walks down the aisle to the old man.

"Thank you, General," she says. "You did wonders. Er... if you don't mind, could you tell me what you said to Billy? I mean, it worked and maybe I could use it again..."

The old guy chuckles and says: "I showed him my pilot's gold wings and my medals and I told him I was a flight commander. I said I was allowed to throw anyone out of any plane at any time, whenever I felt like it."

A thin time of it

A bloke has been having a great time on holiday in Amsterdam, sampling a selection of the sexual delights on offer. Now, though, he's not feeling too well and he goes to see a doctor, who sends him off for some tests.

When the results are back, the bloke is called back to the surgery, and the doctor doesn't seem too happy with what he's reading.

"Well, sir," he says after a moment, "according to these tests, you're suffering from syphilis, leprosy and Aids."

"Oh, my God! What can I do?"

"Not a lot, unfortunately," the doctor replies. "All I can suggest is a diet of sole, pizzas and pancakes."

"Sorry? You think Aids can be cured with pancakes?" the patient asks, surprised.

"Eh? Oh, no! I was just thinking what kind of food can easily be slid under the door of a hospital room."

Isn't that amazing?

A pair of Americans are in the Gare du Nord in Paris, waiting to board their train. Bored, they take a stroll around and notice a strange little machine with a seat and a coin slot. They look around for some instructions but find none. Shrugging, the first Yankee climbs on the seat and feeds a euro into the slot. Clicking noises are heard and after a few seconds a strip of paper is ejected from another slot. On it is written: "Your name is Alex Smith, you are American, you are 39, you weigh 80 kilos and you are boarding the 10.43 train to Luxembourg."

"Wow, this is fantastic!" the bloke exclaims. "I didn't know the French were so technologically advanced. It puts us to shame."

His companion agrees and decides to have a go. He climbs on the seat, pays the machine and, sure enough, out comes a slip of paper. "Your name is George Jones, you are an American citizen with traces of Cherokee blood, you are 42, you weigh 78 kilos and you are boarding the 10.43 train to Luxembourg."

"Amazing," he says. "I wonder how they do that?" In a bid to confuse the machine and get to the bottom of it, they decide to swap clothes quickly and do another test. They swap jackets, baseball caps, sunglasses and shoes, and the first tourist climbs on the seat again. A third euro brings the result: "Your name is still Alex Smith, you are still a 39-year-old American weighing 80 kilos and if you carry on being silly you and your friend George Jones are going to miss the 10.43 to Luxembourg, which is ready to depart now."

For one night only

Two young people hiking in the mountains find themselves stranded at nightfall and take shelter in a refuge. There's no way they can trek down to the village in this blizzard; they'll have to sleep here, alone – in the same bed.

Night falls and they turn in. The girl has a crafty peek at the bloke getting undressed and she's quite impressed. She's lying there thinking indecent thoughts, and eventually nudges the guy.

"I'm not used to sleeping on the left side of the bed. Do you mind me sleeping on your side?" she asks in a little voice. "All you have to do is slide along above me; I'll slide underneath."

"No, it's OK," the guy says. He gets up, walks around to the other side of the bed and surrenders the left side. The girl's frustrated and feeling like a fool. Lust is fighting with pride and, after a little while, lust wins.

"After all," she says, "I didn't realise that there's a draught on this side. Would you mind me going back to the left side of the bed again? There's no need for you to get up in the cold, though; just pass over me and I'll slide under you."

"No, no problem; I'll move." The guy once again gets up, walks to the other side and gets back into bed.

"What's the matter with you?" the girl shouts, incensed. "Don't you understand what I want?"

"Oh, I understand all right," the guy replies, "but there's no way you're going to get all of the bed!"

Roll over, Beethoven

A tourist is sightseeing near Vienna. She comes upon the grave of Beethoven and begins reading the commemorative plaque, only to be distracted by a low scratching noise, as if something were rubbing against a piece of paper. She collars a passing native and asks what the scratching sound is. The local replies: "Oh, that's Beethoven. He's decomposing."

Just so we're clear...

A couple in their late fifties met a few months earlier and are now getting ready to marry in Las Vegas. They want this relationship to go smoother than their previous ones, so they decide to talk things through before signing any papers.

As each of them owns a house, they decide to sell both and each pay half on a new house. This seems reasonable and their feeling of mutual trust is heightened. Things go smoothly regarding household expenses and groceries. They're not big eaters and they should be able to split the bills in two every month.

On a more personal basis, the bride-to-be asks her suitor what he wants to do about sex, to which he replies: "Oh, infrequently." She looks at him, frowns and asks: "Is that one word or two?"

In wad we trust

What is the most common speech impediment when on holiday in America? Chewing gum.

Capisce?

What do you get when you cross a Mafia lieutenant and a German tourist?

Someone who makes you an offer you can't understand.

Superior wisdom

A group of nuns has been sent to a needy parish in Africa. The Mother Superior of the convent has organised an information session about what the locals are like and how to make sure the sisters are safe when going out.

The session goes well and it's now question time. A little mouse of a nun raises her hand.

"Mother Superior, what should we do if we get accosted at night by a man with bad intentions?"

"First of all, try to avoid being out of the convent at night," the Mother Superior advises. "But if such a situation arose, I would lift my habit up."

There are little cries of surprise in the audience.

"Lift your habit? But... what would you do then?"

"Next, I would ask the man to drop his trousers."

This time, there are no cries of surprise in the audience – just a shocked silence.

"You see," the Mother Superior continues, "I can run much faster with my habit up than any man can with his trousers down."

Nun but the lonely heart

A nun and a priest are in the desert on a holiday excursion. They get lost and end up huddling together beside their dying camel, using its body to protect them from the sun. They pray, they chant, they perform all kinds of devotional exercises, but God seems to be busy elsewhere and doesn't come to their rescue.

They're going to die.

Before they die, though, the priest decides he wants a favour from the nun. "Sister," he says. "I've never seen a woman naked. I mean, as we're going to die, I'd like to see a woman without her clothes on at least once in my life."

The nun thinks it over and agrees. When she's naked, she says: "Come to think of it, Father, I haven't seen a man naked either."

The priest nods and he, too, takes his clothes off.

"Father, what's this thing dangling between your legs?" the nun enquires curiously.

"This, my child is a gift from God. I put it in you and I create life."

"Forget about me," the nun exclaims hopefully. "Stick it in the camel!"

Accident of birth

Bu, Chu and Fu are three Chinese friends who are visiting America. They love the country so much that they want to stay and live there. The immigration officer says that's fine, as long as they vow to abide by American law and the American way of life. This also means that they have to change their names. They all agree. Bu changes his name into Buck. Chu changes his name into Chuck. Fu goes back to China.

I feel your pain

A British man is visiting New Orleans in the aftermath of the hurricane. He walks around, witnessing the ravages the natural disaster has caused to the city, and goes to see the head of the fire department to congratulate him on the tremendous job his team has done.

"Well, thank you, sir. Say, I can tell you're not from these parts, are you?"

"No; I'm from Wolverhampton."

"And what state is that in?"

"Oh, roughly as bad as this, I reckon."

An honest mistake

The seven dwarves are in Italy for a fortnight, having left Sleeping Beauty at home with the washing-up, the laundry and the ironing. They visit the various sites and end up in Rome, in Vatican City, for a private audience with the Pope. They are all impressed by the old man, especially Grumpy, who takes him aside and bombards him with questions.

"Tell me, Your Holiness; do you have nuns here?"

"We don't have any nuns working here, but they come and visit, yes."

"Do you have small nuns?"

"Small nuns?" the pontiff asks, puzzled.

"Yeah, about my height: maybe a bit smaller, even."

"I'm sorry; no. I don't think we employ nuns that small."

"You've never met a dwarf nun, then?"

"No, I haven't. I can ask my staff to have a look, but I'm pretty positive there aren't any dwarf nuns."

Grumpy leaves with a worried look on his face. As soon as they're out of the palace, he is surrounded by the other dwarves.

"So what did he say? What did he say?" the other dwarves ask.

"He said there weren't any dwarf nuns," Grumpy replies forlornly.

The others start chanting: "Grumpy fucked a penguin; Grumpy fucked a penguin!"

The pitiless dessert

A plane crashes in the desert and only two men survive out of 300 passengers. They take with them all the water and food they can and begin trekking through the desert, hoping to find civilisation. Soon the water runs out and there they are, filthy and ragged, at the mercy of circling vultures. Suddenly, one of them sees something shimmering in the heat haze, some way off. They start to run and reach a sort of market with three or four tents.

"Water, please!" they croak to the first Arab, their throats parched. "Do you sell water?"

"Sorry; I've only got whipped cream," he replies.

The men tumble into the next tent and again ask for water. "Sorry; I only have custard," says the Arab sitting within.

They go into the last tent and ask for water, but again are disappointed: "I've only got jelly. Sorry."

As the men resume their desert trek, one turns to the other and remarks: "That was weird: all that food, and no water."

"Yes," the other replies. "It was a trifle bazaar."

A tight spot

A plane crashes in a rocky desert somewhere. Everybody dies but a Scot, who staggers out of the wreckage and stumbles into a cave. The Red Cross is alerted to the crash and turns up a few days later. The team searches the area but there is nothing to be found but wreckage and slowly decomposing bodies.

"There are some caves over there," one of the search leaders says. "Let's go and check them out."

A group of volunteers starts climbing towards the caves, shouting for any survivors to make themselves known.

"Who's there?" the Scot asks in a feeble voice when they get near his cave.

"There's somebody in there!" the volunteer shouts. "It's the Red Cross, sir."

"I gave already," the Scot shouts back.

Salad days

A lone woman is on holiday in the south of Italy: warm weather, fantastic scenery, great food – everything's perfect. She's renting a little cottage with a garden attached and, in the first week of her stay, she potters about in the vegetable patch. One day she notices how red the neighbour's tomatoes are.

"Antonio, how do you get such healthy-looking tomatoes?" she asks him. "Mine just refuse to ripen."

"Ah, it's not complicated, Signora," Antonio replies, his crinkled face split in a grin. "Every morning I get naked in front of them and they blush prettily."

"I see," the woman says. It isn't something she'd usually do back in London, but she's on holiday and so she decides to try it out.

A few days later, Antonio peers above the little fence separating the two gardens and sees the English tourist in a deckchair, reading a book.

"Any luck with the tomatoes, Signora?" he asks.

She replies with a wink: "No, my tomatoes are just as green as before, but have a look at the size of this cucumber!"

First things first

A family man is driving at a reasonable speed through the stunning vistas of America's Wild West when he witnesses an accident. A lorry driver is overtaking a brand-new Buick when he swervesd to the right unexpectedly and scrapes the entire side of the car. Both the car and the lorry stop and the family man decides to stop too, in case they need a witness statement.

"Look at that!" the drive of the Buick is screaming. "A brand-new Buick! I've only had it two weeks! I'm a lawyer and let me tell you, you're in deep shit, man."

The family man is astounded to see such a materialistic person. He approaches the lawyer and says: "Stop worrying about the car; think about yourself. You had your elbow out of the window; can't you see the truck just ripped your arm off?"

The lawyer looks at the guy, then at his missing arm, and wails: "Oh, my God: my Rolex!"

A bit flaky

Two old codgers suffering from Alzheimer's are on the promenade, trying to decide what ice cream to order.

"Chocolate," says the first one. "I want chocolate ice cream."

"Right. Chocolate." His friend gets up from the bench they're sitting on.

"Oh: and a flake too."

"A flake?"

"Yeah, you know: a chocolate biscuit thing."

"You want a biscuit?"

"No, just a flake"

"A flake."

"On a chocolate ice cream."

"Right."

"And some strawberry sauce too."

"I'll never remember that," groans the other, holding his head in his hands.

"Yeah, you will. It's easy: chocolate ice cream with a flake and some strawberry sauce."

"Right."The old man shuffles off and is swallowed up by the crowd.

Half an hour later he's back. "What do you call that?" shouts his friend.

"A bag of chips."

"And where's my kebab?"

Under his spell

Ladies, what do you get that's long and hard if you marry a Greek?
A surname.

Natural remedy

A European couple are on holiday in Africa. They're chatting with a few locals by the water pump when a man walks up to them. He lifts his hand in greeting but, before he actually talks to them, he grabs a passing monkey and kisses it smack on the arse.

"Why did you do that?" the woman blurts out without thinking.

"That's because I have chapped lips," the man replies.

"Is that a local cure for chapped lips?" the woman enquires.

"Man, no, but it sure stops me from licking them."

I'm glad you asked me that...

A young camel has reached the age when young camels ask loads of questions about the world and themselves.

"Mum, tell me; why do I have these weird-shaped feet with three toes?"

"That's to help you walk on the treacherous desert sand, darling. It makes you much more stable on this kind of terrain than any other animal," his mum answers.

The little camel ponders this for a while and comes up with another question.

"Tell me; why is it I have such long eyelashes?"

"That's to keep the sand out of your eyes, honey. When the desert wind howls, they'll keep the sand away."

Fair enough, the little camel thinks, marvelling at the sheer beauty of the engineering of eyelashes.

"Tell me, mum; why do we have these great big lumps on our backs?"

"These big lumps will hoard water for days, so that we can live in the desert without dehydrating."

The little camel thinks it over and finally asks: "Mum, what exactly are we doing in London Zoo?"

The apes of froth

If you go on holiday in Borneo, you might come across an animal that's white, fluffy, very sweet and lives in trees. It's called a meringue-utan.

One of those days

The plane has landed safely and the captain is addressing the passengers: "We're now in Liverpool. The temperature outside is 17 degrees, the sky is clear and the day promises to be mild. I hope you enjoyed the flight and that you will travel with us again soon. Thank you and good morning."

The passengers are starting to unbuckle their seatbelts when they realise the captain has forgotten to switch off the PA system: "Right. I'm off for a shit; then I'm gonna shag the new stewardess."

The passenger and the crew stand horrified as a young and lovely hostess, her cheeks flaming, rushes towards the cockpit. Just as she's about to open the door in outrage, an elderly woman stops her and says: "Don't be too eager for your shag, honey. He said he needed to go for a shit first."

Lack of transparency

Snow White has been back a few days from a wild weekend break in Ibiza with the dwarves and heads off to the camera shop where she dropped off her negatives to be processed.

"I'm sorry, Miss, but there'll be a slight delay," the assistant apologises. "I don't know what happened: maybe a problem with the processing. I can't really tell you when I'm going to get them."

Snow White's shoulders slump and, as she does every time she's experiencing strong emotions, she burst into song: "One day, my prints will come!"

Pastry-faced?

A woman has booked a holiday in a campsite. She learns that it's a tradition on the site to hold a last-day-of-summer Naked Beach Bash, where everyone is naked and they all go skinny-dipping. She's a bit concerned about this, but as the end of summer approaches she realises that people are rather friendly and not at all leery or intimidating. Actually, everyone's very polite to her and to everyone else, as if this skinny-dipping thing was just another social event. She does notice, however, that one man seems to be admired more than any other by all the women on the site. She also notices that there's a woman, quiet-looking and unprepossessing, who seems to be this bloke's particular favourite. She enquires about them to her neighbour in the tent next door.

"Oh, yeah; the bloke is Michel. He comes here every year."

"And everybody likes him because he's French?"

"Oh, not only that," her neighbour says, biting her lip. "You should see him at the Naked Beach Bash. He can hold two cups of tea and nine doughnuts."

"What about the woman?" she asks, eyeing Michel speculatively from the corner of her eye.

"That's Sally. She's the only one of us who can eat the last doughnut."

The local baa

What do you call a sheep tied to a lamp-post in Wales?
A leisure centre.

Sudden impact

A young couple go out for a drive one evening. On the way, the man says to the girl, "If I go at 100 miles an hour, will you take off your clothes?" She agrees and he begins to speed up. When the speedometer hits a ton, she starts to strip. When she gets all her clothes off he's so busy staring at her that he drives off the road and flips the car.

The girl is thrown clear without a scratch, but her clothes and her boyfriend are trapped in the car.

"Go and get help!" he pleads.

"I can't," she replies, "I'm naked."

He points to his shoe, which has been thrown from the car, and says, "Cover your snatch with that and go and get some help!"

So she takes his shoe, covers herself up and runs to the petrol station down the road. When she arrives she's frantic, and yells to the attendant, "Help me! My boyfriend's trapped!"

The attendant looks down at the shoe and replies, "I'm sorry, miss. He's too far in."

Quick thinking

A couple have been renting the same cottage every year for five years, next to another couple who've also been renting their cottage for five years. They have become friends of sorts and often arrange picnics or barbecues together.

One year John notices that his neighbour Alan is wearing an earring. This surprises him, as people who rent the same cottage five years in a row aren't usually the type to wear earrings. On the contrary, Alan has always come across as rather traditionalist.

Their wives having gone to the local shop together, John takes the opportunity to tackle Alan about the whole earring thing.

"I didn't know you were into earrings."

"Well... I am," Alan replies, a bit sheepishly.

"How long have you been wearing one?"

"Er... ever since my wife found it in the bed."

Working her passage

A young woman is sitting in a pub on her own. She seems pretty fed-up and rather down. She is staring at her half-empty glass, fidgeting with a mobile phone. A guy has been checking her out and finally decides to go and talk to her.

"How are you doing?" he asks. "You don't look happy; is something bothering you?"

The woman is about to retort that it's none of his business when her loneliness gets the better of her and she starts pouring out the story of her life. After half an hour listening to one emotional disaster after another, the bloke strokes his chin and says: "I know what you need: a change of scenery. I work on a ocean liner. I can smuggle you to America in the back of my van and put you up in my place over there."

"Really?"

"It'll work, if we're quiet about it."

The young woman hasn't got much to lose, so she agrees. They're on the move for a couple of hours and then the van stops. She hears foreign voices shouting commands and then feels the unmistakable sway of the sea and hears the sighing of the waves.

The man opens the back of the van surreptitiously and quickly takes her to a little room. There's just enough space to lie down, and they make love.

This goes on for some time. The woman isn't bothered: the guy brings her food and sometimes a book. She can use the cabin's basic toilet and washing facilities. At regular intervals the bloke turns up and they have sex, which is fine too.

She's been in her little cubicle for a few days when the door suddenly bursts open. An older man in uniform is staring at her.

"So, what have we here? A stowaway?" he demands.

The girl pleads: "I was just fed-up with the world, and I met this guy. He promised to take me to America. In return, he screws me."

"He certainly does, young lady," the captain replies. "This is the Dover-Calais ferry."

Eau de Odour

A woman, not overly bright (possibly a blonde, even) is trying out the fragrances in the duty-free shop aboard the Calais-Dover ferry. She sniffs at a bottle with the name 'Viens à moi'.

"Viens à moi? What on earth does that mean?" she exclaims.

"That's French," a salesperson says helpfully. "It means 'Come to me.'"

The woman turns to her friend. "'Come to me'? It doesn't smell like come to me. Does it smell like come to you?"

Fetch!

What do you call a boomerang that doesn't come back?
A stick.

This really happened to a friend of mine

This guy has been trying to use the plane's toilets for an hour, but they're always full.

"I really need to go," he says to the flight attendant. "The male toilets are always engaged. Please, please let me use the ladies'. I promise I won't be long!"

"OK," she says after a minute considering the guy's plight, "but you'll have to promise not to touch anything."

The guy promises and is allowed in the female toilets.

He sits down on the seat and has the longest piss of his life. He then notices three buttons on the wall. The plane being one of these brand-new, gadget-packed affairs, he wonders what the buttons are for. He absently-mindedly presses the first. A gentle spray of lavender-scented water cleans his arse.

After the initial shock, he finds the experience rather nice, so he presses the button again. Then, overcome with curiosity, he presses the second. A fine dusting of talcum powder is puffed on his balls. This is so cute! He bursts out laughing and soon the air is thick with talcum powder. Settling back in the seat, he considers the third button and his promise not to touch anything.

What the hell... He presses the last button.

He wakes up in hospital. He's lying in bed, his legs strapped in a sling and his groin hurting like mad. The flight attendant is sitting next to him.

"Where am I?" he asks.

"You had to press the last button, didn't you?" she asks him. "We had to make an emergency landing for you, you know."

"Yes, yes; I did press the bloody button. What happened?"

"It was the tampon removal button. You'll find your balls under your pillow."

Pianissimo

How do you shut an Italian up?
Tie his arms behind his back.

From beyond the grave

A geek has gone to Florida, for a geek meeting. His geek girlfriend is staying home, although she's scheduled to join him the following day. The geek gets off the plane, finds a hotel, books a room and walks to the nearest internet café. He types a message to his girlfriend but, as luck would have it, he misspells her email address and his message is instead sent to the widow of a priest who's died recently.

On the other side of the world, the poor woman hears a chime coming from her computer. She checks her mail, reads the message, lets out a horrified scream and keels over, dead.

Her daughter, alerted by the noise, rushes in to find her mum dead and a strange message on the screen.

"Dearest,
Just checked in. Everything prepared for your arrival tomorrow.
PS. Sure is hot down here."

Land of plenty

An American tourist walks into a butcher's shop in Moscow.

"Good morning; I don't suppose you have any bread?" he asks.

"Ah; you are mistaken, my tourist friend; here we don't have any meat," the butcher replies.

Vladimir Ilyich Linen

What does a Russian use to wipe his mouth after dinner?

A Soviet.

Every picture tells a story

A couple are visiting the American West. They end up in a small town, where the only attraction is a museum dedicated to Colonel Custer and the war against the Indians. Deciding that they've driven enough for the day, they book a room in the local hotel, have a quick shower and head for the museum. The museum is rather quaint and the main attraction is a large mural depicting a cow sporting a halo and a multitude of Indians portrayed in various sexual positions. The couple stare at it for a while, trying to make sense of it, but finally they give up and go and ask someone.

"Er..." the husband says to the pretty clerk at the information desk. "We've just been to see your mural, you know, and we were wondering... I mean, what does it represent?"

The girl laughs and replies: "The mural represents what Colonel Custer thought moments before he died. The title is: 'Holy cow, look at all these fucking Indians!'"

Piles of snow

A word of advice if you're planning a holiday in the north of Sweden. Be careful not to sit too long on the ice. If you do, you'll get polaroids.

Boxer dog?

A guy is returning home after an out-of-town business trip. He's left quite quickly and hasn't been able to say goodbye to his little girl, so he wants to make amends by getting her a present. He's bought her a puppy but, not wanting to have to go through all the paperwork needed to take an animal on a plane, he's just tucked the puppy down his trousers.

Everything's going according to plan until a flight attendant notices him shuddering and squirming in his seat.

"Are you all right, sir?"

"Yes; no problem," the guy replies with a weird smile.

The attendant leaves him alone for a while, until she notices that he's not only still squirming and shuddering in his seat, but now moaning and gurgling.

"Come on, sir," she says. "What's the matter? I've been doing this job long enough to know that you're not comfortable."

"Well," the guy says, blushing, "I have to confess something to you. I didn't want to waste time filling out the paperwork and chance missing the flight, so I put a little puppy in my trousers. It's a present for my daughter."

"Oh, I see," the attendant says with a smile. "He's not housetrained, right?"

"Oh, it's not that. He's not weaned yet."

This island earth

An engineer has booked a cruise. He's learning to relax by spending time lying in a deckchair, forcing his mind not to wonder how a deckchair actually works and resolutely avoiding taking it apart and building it back up again. After a week, he's finally getting into some serious chilling-out when the liner's hit by the mother of all storms. As the ship slowly starts to sinks the engineer, miraculously, manages to hold on to a lifebelt. He drifts for days, until he's washed up on a sandy beach, and his new life begins.

Seven years later the engineer is still on his island, living on a meagre diet of fruit and the occasional barbecued fish. He's given up hope of ever being rescued when a small rowing boat appears on the horizon. The boat soon reaches the beach and a beautiful woman jumps into the shallows and hauls the boat to shore.

"Hello," she says.

The man is too surprised to answer.

"Were you on the liner too?" she asks him gently.

"Yeah, yeah; that was seven years ago," he finally replies.

"Yes, it's been a long time. I washed up on the next island. It took me a while to build this boat."

"How did you do it?"

"I used palm tree bark and eucalyptus," she replies. "I bonded the inner and the outer skins with some resin from a gum tree. I made the oars with palm branches."

"But where did you get the tools?" enquires the engineer, running a hand along the gunwale approvingly.

"Well, there's a rich vein of iron on the island I come from. I managed to build a fire hot enough to melt some of the ore. I used rocks to hammer the lumps into shape and got myself a set of rudimentary tools."

"That's amazing," the man says, truly impressed.

"What about you?" she asks him. Pointing to a lopsided

arrangement of sticks, creepers and leaves, she asks, "Is that your shelter?"

"Erm... I must confess, I haven't really started yet: you know, I mean, I've been pretty depressed since the disaster and I kind of lost it for a bit," he explains lamely.

"I understand," says the woman, patting his arm. "I went through a very difficult time myself." She looks around and then says: "Maybe we could go back to my place; it should be more comfortable."

The man agrees and she rows him to the next island.

There, sheltered from the wind, is a beautiful little bungalow painted blue with a verandah, an outside toilet, a small garden at the back and lush bushes of exotic flowers growing around the house.

"It's not much, but I like to call it home," the woman says modestly. She invites him to sit in a cane chair and fusses over the feather-filled cushions.

"Would you like a drink?" she offers.

"Er, yeah: sure," the engineer replies, astounded at the comfort and ingenuity of the place.

A few minutes later, the woman hands him a glass of an amber liquid. The engineer sips cautiously and realises he's drinking a piña colada.

"How did you build all this?" he asks, waving to the bungalow, the patio, the vegetable patch and finally his cocktail.

"Well, it's taken me quite a while, really," she explains. "I built the house with palm branches I wove together. I used the waste of a kind of wild pig living around here. The droppings are easy to work with and they're pretty strong when dry. Of course I was a bit squeamish at first, but it was worth it," she says with a little laugh. "Once the house was built, I had time on my hands to try glass-blowing – after all, glass is only melted sand, when you think of it. I designed a set of wine glasses; then I made some ceramic plates in my kiln."

"This is astonishing," the man whispers. He smacks his lips in appreciation. "And this isn't half bad," he says, squinting at the liquid in his glass.

"Exotic moonshine," the woman says, obviously proud at the man's praise. "Once I could get a hot enough fire going, it was easy to get some glass and build an alembic. This is only fermented coconut milk and fruit juice. But enough of this," she says. "Just relax and enjoy yourself. I'm going to slip into something more comfortable."

She disappears into the house and reappears a few minutes later dressed in a practically see-through gown woven of palm fibres and smelling very sweet. She has rouged her cheeks lightly and is absolutely ravishing.

"I know I'm being a bit forward," she asks, "but, you know, is there anything you really missed while you were alone on your beach? Something all men and women need to feel alive and loved? Maybe something that'd be very nice to do now?" she continues suggestively.

The man looks at her with bulging eyes. "Yes; there's something I've been wanting to do for a long time, but it's impossible," he breathes.

"What is it? Nothing's impossible," she purrs.

The man leans forward and, in an awed tone, asks: "Don't tell me you've knocked up a set of golf clubs too!"

Pilot error

A young prankster of a pilot feels like some fun so, just before landing at night, he keys his radio mike and says: "Guess who?" The air traffic controller, fed-up with his practical jokes, turns all the airfield's lights off and replies: "Guess where!"

No such thing as a free lunch

A company director is taking two of his employees to lunch, as part of a move to secure workers' loyalty. On the table in the restaurant is a tarnished old lamp. As the first employee, a software engineer, reaches over for the complimentary toothpicks, he accidentally brushes it with his sleeve. What is supposed to happen happens, and a genie pops out of the lamp in a wreath of fragrant smoke.

"Thank you for letting me out of my prison," the genie says to them with a bow. "I shall grant you three wishes." He looks around at the three men and says: "Well, to be fair, I think I should grant one wish to each of you."

They agree; the software engineer thinks for a minute and says: "I'd like to be cruising around the world in a yacht with an all-woman crew."

"As you wish," the genie says, and the software engineer disappears in a puff of smoke.

The second employee, a project manager, says: "I'd like to be riding a Harley in Arizona, followed by a posse of female bikers." The genie nods and the project manager likewise disappears in a puff of smoke. The genie turns to the company director and enquires: "And what will your wish be?"

The guy looks at the genie sternly and replies: "Make sure they're back tomorrow at nine."

Shut up and eat it

Due to harsh competition, an air travel company has decided to review its in-flight food policy. As a consequence, this is what an air hostess said to a passenger at mealtime:

"Would you like dinner, sir?" she asks.
"What are my choices?" the passenger replies.

"Yes or no."

Just do it

An airline pilot is running late for his date. His first flight was cancelled this morning and now technical problems are delaying his departure. Sitting in the cockpit waiting for clearance, he texts his girlfriend and tells her he's going to try to make up for lost time.

Clearance is finally given and the plane takes off. The pilot is fuming at the delay, but you can't really go over the speed limit in an airplane, so all he can do is grind his teeth. However, half-way through the flight he gets a call from an air traffic controller which leaves him incensed.

"What? You want me to turn due south? Do you know how much time this new route will add to my flight? I've wasted enough time today as it is already. What's the reason for this change of route, anyway?"

"Noise reduction measures."

The pilot is speechless for a second, then roars: "What? Are you telling me I have to waste even more time because some pedestrian 25,000 feet below might hear me?"

"Apparently, Captain, you've never heard two 747s collide," the air traffic controller replies coolly.

Bloody foreigners

A Swiss man is lost in the Australian Outback. He slows down and approaches two Aussies waiting for a hypothetical bus.

"Entschuldigung; können Sie Deutsch sprechen?" he asks.

The two Aussies just stare at him.

"Excusez-moi; parlez-vous Francais?" the guy tries then.

The two continue to stare.

"Parlete Italiano?"

More staring.

"Hablan ustedes Español?"

Still nothing.

There follows a few minutes of silence during which the two Aussies just blankly stare and the Swiss guy just shakes his head in disgust. As the bloke drives off, one of the Aussies remarks: "Y'know, maybe I should have learned a foreign language."

"What for?" the other asks. "It didn't do that bloke any good, did it?"

Well, you would, wouldn't you?

What did the cannibal do after he dumped his girlfriend?
He wiped his arse.

That sounds familiar

A woman calls the travel agent to make a reservation. Apparently she wants to go to Hippopotamus, in America.

The assistant at the other end of the line is baffled. He's never heard of a town called Hippopotamus. He puts the woman on hold and checks with his supervisor. The supervisor frantically searches through an atlas but, try as he might, he can't find Hippopotamus on the map.

"Are you sure of the name of the town, madam?" he asks the client.

"Of course I am," she replies.

"It's just that I can't find any information about Hippopotamus. I can't find this town anywhere. It's not listed."

"Oh, come on, now; it's quite a famous American town."

The clerk thinks about it and then slowly says: "Do you mean Buffalo?"

"That's the one! I knew it was a big animal."

Bags sit here

A man is trying to fit loads of personal luggage around his aircraft seat and in the overhead rack. He's taking a long time and the flight attendant is explaining to him that his luggage constitutes a hazard and will have to be transferred to the hold.

The passenger grumbles: "I don't have this problem when I travel with other airlines."

The flight attendant, without missing a beat, replies: "When you travel with other airlines, I don't have this problem either."

Hold very tight, please

A blonde and two brunettes are down in London for the weekend. They decide to get on a sightseeing bus and visit all the famous places. Unfortunately, there are only two seats free on the bottom and one on the top deck. The brunettes decide to let the blonde have the top seat and to remain together on the lower level.

The trip starts and soon the guide has all the tourists enthralled by bits and pieces of history. After a while, everybody is singing old English songs and having a thoroughly good time.

One of the brunettes decides to go and see how the blonde's doing. To her surprise, she's sitting on the edge of her seat, clinging on to the back of the seat in front for dear life and looking paralysed with fear.

"What's the matter with you?" the brunette asks. "We're having a grand time downstairs; we're all singing and laughing and all!"

"Yeah," the blonde says between clenched teeth, "but you have a driver."

Mother tongue

An American tourist in England is asking the hotel receptionist where the elevator is.

"The what, sir?"

"The elevator."

The receptionist looks at the Yank blankly for a few seconds and then nods: "You mean the lift," he says with a smile.

"No; I mean the elevator," the American bloke repeats, irritated.

"Well, over here we call them lifts."

"Listen here, fella," the Yank grunts. "I call it an elevator because someone in America invented the elevator."

"That's true, sir," the receptionist replies politely, "but someone here in England invented the English language."

Pole position

A bloke has made the terrible mistake of falling asleep in the sun and now his legs are terribly sunburnt. He goes to the GP.

"I'm sorry; there's not a lot I can do for you. Try cold water and some Viagra at night."

"Viagra? Why Viagra?"

"It'll keep the bedsheets away from your skin."

Cross my palm

A man is having his palm read. The gypsy looks deeply into his eyes and says: "I see that you're the father of two boys."

"That's what you think," the man says. "I'm the father of *three* boys."

"That's what *you* think," the woman sneers.

Close to his family

There's this man who's very, very stingy. At the height of summer, he says to his kids: "If you're good boys, I'll show you a picture of someone eating ice cream."

Johnny Rotten

Two men are striking up a conversation on a plane.
   "And what do you do for a living?" the first one asks.
   "I manage a company that deals with rubber products."
   "Rubber products? What kind?"
   "We make teats and condoms."
   "Isn't that a strange combination?" the guy asks.
   "Well, no; you see, basically a teat's built like a condom, only it's thicker. Here," the other man says, taking a packet of condoms from his pocket. "Here's a sample of our best-quality condoms."
   The other passenger, not used to being offered condoms by another man, picks up the packet gingerly, opens it and inspects the condoms.
   "But there's a hole at the end of this one!" he exclaims, horrified.
   "Oh yes," the manager replies with a smile. "One out of every three condoms has a hole in it."
   "Don't you think that's a bit irresponsible?"
   "Oh, I agree: but it's very good for the teat market."

Safety first

A couple are driving along amid the magnificent scenery of southern France when the wife says to her husband: "We've been married five years, but now I want a divorce."

The husband says nothing, but increases his speed.

"I've been seeing your friend Andy for over a year now and I want to go and live with him."

The husband remains silent and increases his speed. He's now reached 75mph.

"He's far better in bed than you are," the wife carries on, trying to goad her husband into some rash statement she can use against him in court. The husband, however, remains silent, only increasing his speed to 85mph. The tyres start screeching on the hairpins.

"I want the house, the kids and the credits cards. What do you want?" the woman asks, clutching the overhead handle.

"I don't want anything; I have everything I need," the man replies, driving now at over 95mph.

"What do you mean? What have you got?"

"The airbag."